The Conscious Entrepreneur

A GUIDE TO MAXIMIZING YOUR POTENTIAL FOR SUCCESS, FREEDOM, AND HAPPINESS

Laura C. Cannon

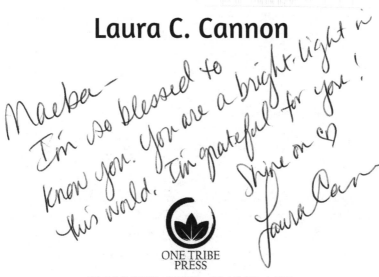

Maeba—
I'm so blessed to know you. You are a bright, light in this world. I'm grateful for you! Shine on ♥
Laura Can

ONE TRIBE
PRESS

ELLICOTT CITY, MARYLAND

One Tribe Press
PO Box 2414
Ellicott City, MD 21041-2414
onetribepress.com
Email: info@onetribepress.com

Book Layout ©2013 BookDesignTemplates.com

Ordering Information:
Quantity sales. Special discounts are available on quantity purchases by corporations, associations, and others. For details, contact the "Special Sales Department" at the address above.

The Conscious Entrepreneur / Laura C. Cannon. —1st ed.
ISBN 978-0-9965586-0-0

PRAISE FOR *THE CONSCIOUS ENTREPRENEUR*

"Companies with a higher sense of purpose outperform others by 400%. In this succinct guide, Laura C. Cannon shows you how to find and use your purpose, and helps entrepreneurs realize their potential, transform their businesses and create more happiness in the world."

> — Jenn Lim, CEO and Co-Founder of Delivering Happiness, Consultant at Zappos.com

"To succeed in business, entrepreneurs first need to develop themselves. *The Conscious Entrepreneur* shares concrete insights that will help you transform your life and achieve true greatness, both personally and professionally."

> — Dorie Clark, author of *Reinventing You* and *Stand Out*

"Laura C. Cannon expertly serves up the 'secret sauce' that sets the world's greatest entrepreneurs apart, and shows you how to pour it on yourself with six foundational concepts of higher-level thinking and learning."

> — Christine Hassler, best-selling author of *Expectation Hangover*

"Wow, I felt like Laura C. Cannon was talking directly to me about success and finding my own true place. It's not new-age dreaming, it's practical advice we can all use."

> — Alan Berg, Certified Speaking Professional® and Business Guru

"As entrepreneurs, we are tasked to be everything to everyone. It's a part of the process and most of us go along with the flow, never really asking ourselves how to make things less stressful or more enjoyable for us and our well-being.

In her new book, *The Conscious Entrepreneur: A Guide to Maximizing Your Potential for Success, Freedom, and Happiness*, Laura C. Cannon fluently translates those thoughts into actionable items with candid insights and excellent questions that every entrepreneur - no matter what level - should address.

Owning a business enterprise is hard. Running a business enterprise takes skill. But it also requires heart and as noted in the book, all entrepreneurs need to follow their "inner compass" because that gut feeling will always steer you to the place and the situations where you belong, and where you will soar! Kudos to Laura C. Cannon for such a thoughtful soul-searching book!"

> — Linnyette Richardson-Hall, Wedding Planner & Industry Expert and Featured Consultant on Style Network's "*Whose Wedding Is It Anyway?*"

Acknowledgments

I am deeply thankful to Ally Machate of Ally Machate Consulting for her book collaborating skills, support, encouragement, and her extremely vital role in transforming the manuscript into this book in a ridiculously short amount of time.

I am incredibly grateful to all of the amazing souls who have touched my life; their wisdom and teachings will forever reside in my heart. To name just a few: Evan, for all of the things you do for me every day to keep my buckets full, and for making me a mother, your love inspires me daily; my daughter, Satori, for choosing me as your mother and awakening my heart more fully each and every day; Mom and Dad, who have been two amazing examples of the entrepreneurial spirit and always knew the right combination of love and support that was needed.

Tim, for walking this path with me for the past 15 years and for your fierce and unwavering dedication to awakening. Without you, this certainly would not have been possible.

Nicole F., Kim G., every girl should be as lucky to have two best friends like you; Emily B. for her ninja-like grammar skills and friendship; Christina F. and Julie C., for standing in for me so I had the time and support needed to make this a reality; Stephen I., for exploring some of life's greatest mysteries with me; all of the courageous and awesome members of my soul family tribe who contribute so much to the expansion of consciousness on this planet in so many ways.

Profound gratitude goes to all of the teachers and experiences that have helped me to awaken to the wisdom within so that I may be in service to the awakening consciousness of humanity. I am grateful to all of my clients, colleagues, and friends who continue to give me so many opportunities to learn and grow.

Lokah Samastah Sukhino Bhavantu

May all beings everywhere be happy and free, and may the thoughts, words, and actions of my own life contribute in some way to that happiness and to that freedom for all.

Contents

Introduction 11

    A Hierarchy of Needs 14

    The Conscious Entrepreneur 16

    What Self-Actualization Looks Like........................... 19

    Your Business is Your Vehicle 25

    How to Use This Book.. 27

Chapter 1: Oneness.. 31

    You Are Your Business, Your Business Is You......... 35

    Mirror, Mirror... 39

    The Way You Do One Thing is the Way You Do
    Everything... 45

    No Victims Here 48

    Finding Our Way 59

Chapter 2: Presence 61

    The Container of Now... 62

    How We Go Missing.. 68

    It's Never Too Late for Now.. 71

    Creating the Space for Mindfulness........................... 75

    Meditation and Mindfulness—The "Secret" Success
    Formula 78

    Let it Be 83

Chapter 3: Inner Compass 87

    Finding Your Inner Compass 89

    You Are Not Your Thoughts....................................... 93

    The Heart Speaks in Whispers.................................... 97

The Heart Speaks Through the Body..........................99
What Living in the Heart Looks Like.....................107

Chapter 4: Impermanence.................................109

Accepting Impermanence 112
Embracing Impermanence.........................114
Planning for Change....................................118
The Silver Lining of Impermanence.....................127

Chapter 5: Boldness...135

Be Your Own Hero.......................................136
Roadblocks to Boldness.............................137
What Makes Boldness Possible 143
The Two Biggest Pitfalls 149
Risky Business...153
Pushing Your Boundaries 157
Start Now 160

Chapter 6: Service..163

Broadening our Concept of Service 164
A Movement for the Future 169
Leadership Begins with You.....................171
Love is at the Core.....................................173
Act Now...175

Additional Resources...................................179
About the Author 183

I dedicate this book to all those courageous souls who are walking the path of awakening – thank you for your service and love.

Namaste.

Introduction

Not everyone can say they owe their first entrepreneurial success to a sweaty, drunken stranger in a dirty warehouse, but you can't always pick the way these things get started.

After spending over an hour waiting outside in the cold to pay the $10 cover, my friend Dan and I finally made our way inside to see several of our favorite DJs and dance the night away. We were both sophomores in college, and had been looking forward to a hard-earned study break at the end of the fall semester. Eager to get a drink and start dancing, I waited in line for what seemed like forever, only to learn they had already sold out of water. Dan, ever the optimist, convinced me to make my way into the main room—but it was so over-crowded, I could barely move.

As I stood there feeling annoyed and thirsty, the aforementioned stranger added to the ambiance by enthusiastically crashing into me in a vain attempt to dance in such tight quarters. Looking around, I realized there must be at least 500 people in the room and quickly did the math—at ten bucks a head, somebody was having a great night and it sure wasn't me. Standing there with Dan, covered in an intoxicated stranger's sweat, I remember the idea hitting me with near-physical impact. "I could totally host an event, and do it way better than this!" As soon as the words came out of my mouth, I felt it: That surge of energy and inspiration that needs to be birthed into the world. The entrepreneurial spirit had moved me, and I wanted to produce my own event. *I needed to.*

Dan laughed. "If anyone can do it, I'm sure it's you—but I'm also pretty sure you have no idea what you are doing."

He was right. I had absolutely no clue. Although he hadn't intended it as such, I took his comment as a challenge. "Give me three months and I will produce an event way better than this in every way." I have no idea what made me say it, but I as soon as I did I knew I had no choice; I had to make it happen. I started the very next day, making connections, learning the industry, finding a space, booking vendors, starting a legal entity for my business, and raising capital.

Within a few weeks, I had my first incorporated business. Almost three months to the day after that fateful evening, as promised, I hosted my first event: The Secret Garden, an all-night music festival with a line-up of seven of the best regional DJs. It was a success far beyond my wildest imagination. I made a healthy 200% return on the investment and, though it was more than fifteen years ago, people still talk about that night. In fact, just recently someone on Facebook posted a memory of the event and asked if anyone still had a promotional flyer. Through mutual connections the request came my way and since I still had flyers tucked away in an old box, I mailed her one. When she wrote back to thank me, she told me that night changed her life. I feel the same way.

That was the night I caught the entrepreneurial bug, and it bit me hard. I wondered, if I was able to accomplish so much when I knew hardly anything, what could I accomplish if I had more education, more time, more skills, more capital? That night I tapped into a universal human experience—an inner longing to do more, to be better, something that I've since learned to recognize as a need to fulfill my true potential or purpose.

I've had many more successes and created many more businesses since that night, but that feeling lives on in me as it does in so many other entrepreneurs. As creators and risk-takers, entrepreneurs tend to have a unique perspective on the world as something that can be shaped and changed, and the extent of that change is only limited by the potential we choose to develop. I still don't know just how much more I am capable of, but my life is dedicated to exploring the great potential that lives inside of me, and helping others explore theirs as well.

As human beings we have the ability to do many great things in this world, but perhaps the most amazing is the ability to identify and pursue our own unique calling. So many of us want to know through experience what we are truly capable of, to constantly push the boundaries of what's possible for ourselves. Sometimes we experience this type of ambition strongly in our youth, and sometimes it hits us like lightning, out of nowhere, and with great power that can't be ignored. Perhaps you've felt this yearning to align with your own deepest potential and it led you to create a business, a new product, or even to reinvent the business you have. Perhaps you've felt it as a need to discover who you truly are and what your purpose in life (or in business) is. Perhaps you're feeling it right now.

A Hierarchy of Needs

What does that really mean, to fulfill one's potential or purpose? My favorite explanation comes from American psychologist Abraham Maslow, who famously created what many now simply refer to as *Maslow's Hierarchy of Needs*. He described human beings as having basic needs ordered in a hierarchy in which the most pressing needs like the need for food, water, and sleep must be met before one can focus on satisfying needs further up the hierarchy, such as self-esteem and achievement. At the top of this hierarchy is the need to become our most "complete" or "actualized" self. According to Maslow, as we struggle to meet each level of need, we evolve or grow as people, becoming ever more conscious to our inner workings and thereby unlocking our ability to pursue the next level and the next until we reach the top. By the time we get there, the growth that has come as a result of our experiences has helped us achieve a level of consciousness sufficient to support us in self-actualizing. This is how we fulfill our potential: We become the strongest, happiest, most satisfied version of ourselves. We become who we were always meant to be.

Maslow didn't pull this concept entirely out of thin air, however. Through a biographical analysis of people he considered to be examples of self-actualized individuals (people actively living and expressing their full potential)—people like Thomas Jefferson, Eleanor Roosevelt, Frederick Douglass, and Albert Einstein—he found certain personality traits in common that led him to create a profile of the self-actualized human. To be clear, it isn't that these people have reached the top of the pyramid and are now perfect beings. Self-actualization is a living, breathing process; you are never "done." As long as you're alive, you're never going to run out of things that will upset you or provide a new challenge for growth. As I like to say, *life is your guru.*

No matter how evolved you are, no matter how awakened to your full potential, life will always present you with new lessons that require you to practice applying the wisdom you've learned along the way. But when you're operating daily at that level of consciousness, you begin to exhibit certain common, positive traits and join the ranks of what Maslow considered the "self-actualized human beings."

For various reasons having to do with personality, circumstances, and where we fall on Maslow's hierarchy, each of us may choose a different path to self-actualization. For some of us, this path includes leading others in efforts for societal change. For others, it may mean a life of service through volunteering. Entrepreneurship is yet another path of growth that, whether they realize it or not, attracts many people *because* of their deep desire to self-actualize. Many of the traits commonly associated with successful entrepreneurs, such as autonomy, creativity, and a desire to solve some larger problem for their community or even the world, are all included in the findings of Maslow's work.

The Conscious Entrepreneur

At the outset, it may seem like being your own boss is the perfect way to make the kind of schedule that allows you to pursue all of your interests. But what business owner doesn't have a story that involves them working more than forty hours a week, oftentimes even more than seventy? Entrepreneurs are some of the busiest people in the world! Here's where the trap of entrepreneurship comes in: Our desire to self-actualize often drives us to create a business, and yet the obligations that owning a business brings can make it feel almost selfish and indulgent to spend the time on ourselves required to self-actualize! It's all too easy to put aside our need for personal growth when we're faced with staffing emergencies, a huge sales order, lulls in prospect funnels, or a threatened bottom line. Too often, we end up suppressing our desire to grow and to pursue all the benefits of a heightened consciousness to the detriment of both ourselves and our businesses—all in the name of putting our businesses first to reach our entrepreneurial goals.

Though we typically see our personal and professional needs at odds in Western culture, a deeper investigation reveals that they are so intertwined as to be inseparable—and *that's a great thing*. It's great because it means that you don't have to choose; you can satisfy your need for personal growth while satisfying your ambitions for the growth of your business. But how will someone so busy focusing on the external success of their business ever find time to focus on feeding the internal structures supportive of this growth?

It works like this. Your business may take up the majority of your time, but you as a person are the one who is the heart and soul of your business, so when you work on yourself that improvement will naturally come through to your business as well. It's an illusion—one that we'll explore more throughout this book—that your business is something separate from you or from your personal life and that, accordingly, your work to grow professionally is separate from your work to grow personally. I'm not talking about how you allocate your time, or whether you check your email during your family vacation. I'm talking about the fact that, ultimately, when you approach your business from the perspective of the conscious entrepreneur—a business owner who is also dedicated to the practice of greater awareness and personal growth—you can effectively make your business do double duty.

The key is to focus on increasing your level of consciousness. It is only through becoming more conscious and self-aware that you can progress through the hierarchy of needs and develop further along the road to self-actualization. It is also through becoming more conscious that you can join the ranks of entrepreneurial megastars like Oprah, Sir Richard Branson, Arianna Huffington, and Russell Simmons...all of whom attribute their success in large part to living with greater awareness of what's going on both inside and around themselves.

In this book, I'm going to introduce you to some of the best tools to help you to become more conscious and aware all the time. All of them are equally useful to you in your work space and in your personal space, but since your business is what you're devoting most of your time to, you'll find this book a guide to improving and enjoying that time in particular. By focusing on these simple, practical tools and applying them to whatever you are doing, you will be able to transform your journey as an entrepreneur into the journey towards higher consciousness.

The first deliberate step toward self-actualization is recognizing the desire you have to achieve your highest potential. Because you've picked up this book and you're still reading, I'm going to assume that means you're on board—congratulations! You've taken the first step to achieve your highest potential. Now, I'm going to show you where you are already strong, and in which areas you have room to improve, to increase the likelihood that you will be successful at realizing your wildest dreams. You may be much closer than you think.

What Self-Actualization Looks Like

Since we've established that you want to meet your greatest potential, it's important to look at what common characteristics are shared by others who have achieved this state so that we can identify and develop those traits in ourselves. Let's take a look at what Abraham Maslow identified as the characteristics shared by self-actualized, highly conscious individuals.

For each one of the following items, I want you to ask yourself: "To what degree does this characteristic already describe me?" Rate each item on a scale of one to ten, where one means that you have no resonance with the trait at all and ten means that you feel the characteristic defines you explicitly. Be honest with yourself about the areas in which you could grow. As we work through the chapters ahead, you will want to pay special attention to the exercises and ideas associated with the places where you have the most growth to do.

Maslow's Characteristics of the Self-Actualizer

1. *Perception of Reality*: You are comfortable with the truth of *what is* and have more efficient perceptions of the world around you, which helps you be more successful than most at determining truth from falsehood. Because you are generally unthreatened by the uncertainty of life and have a high tolerance for ambiguity, you act in the face of risk and are nimble in business decisions, moving forward even if some aspects of the situation are still unclear.

2. *Acceptance*: You are able to accept yourself, others, and life experiences without much resistance, and yet you are strongly motivated to change those undesirable qualities within yourself that can be changed. You often find yourself looking for training opportunities or projects that push your boundaries. In conflicts or business breakdowns, your first impulse is always to look at how you may have contributed to the situation in a constructive way, without the need to blame yourself or others.

3. *Spontaneity*: You are natural and spontaneous in thought, word, and deed. You don't strain to be or do something just for the effect, but instead find that you feel safe letting the moment dictate your behavior. A supervisor who is competent in this dimension could easily walk into a meeting with an employee who may potentially get fired and allow themselves the space to make their decision live in the moment, as opposed to needing a script.

4. *Problem-Centered*: You focus on the problems of others and society and work actively to find solutions. You're driven by a sense of having a "mission" to help humanity in some way and you generally steer your business with this in mind. It's important to you to "revolutionize" your industry or niche and make things better for everyone.

5. *Solitude*: You have a deep need for solitude and privacy greater than those of the average individual. While you do enjoy the company of others, you are more than comfortable being alone and often times will seek out solitude as a way to recharge. Though you may be drawn to groups that provide a sounding board in the form of an executive board or mastermind group, you will find it necessary to then take time alone to allow your ideas space and room to breathe and develop.

6. *Autonomous*: You are relatively independent of both environment and culture, which means you do not tend to rely on the opinions of others or society when it comes to determining your behavior. You trust yourself completely and are comfortable making decisions alone. This trait is what allows entrepreneurs to create innovative products and services without being concerned for whether they fit the current environment or culture.

7. *Fresh Appreciation*: You have the ability to see the ordinary with a sense of child-like wonder. You meet experiences, people, and events with a fresh curiosity and sincere interest. You are able to fully appreciate things

that most adults pass over, like the beauty of a sunset or the sound of children laughing. Life's simple pleasures bring constant joy to your daily existence.

8. *Mystical or Peak Experiences*: You have had, and continue to have occasionally, peak experiences in which you have a sense of transcendence. This often includes experiencing yourself as one with the universe, nature, or God. Where some seek these experiences out for years without result, or feel lucky to have been "struck" by one, you typically have more of these than most people and the experiences – no matter how they come about – leave a deep impact on your psyche. You tend to frequently experience the feeling of "being in the flow" and it isn't difficult for you to reach or identify this state.

9. *Human Kinship*: You are able to identify with the feelings of others and experience empathy, sympathy, and love for your fellow humans with ease. Because of this, you have a strong desire to help the human race. You see the world and your business in particular as an opportunity to help lift others up right along with you.

10. *Interpersonal Relations*: You have a small number of very close friends to whom you are deeply connected and prefer it this way, rather than having a huge social network. Your approach to referrals is to take the time to get to know a few business contacts very well rather than handing out cards at a networking event. Not the type to hold a grudge, self-actualizers are capable of greater love based on their unbiased perceptions and acceptance of others.

11. *Democratic Values:* This is how Maslow captured the traits of humility and respect toward all human beings regardless of race, creed, sexual orientation, income level, class, religion, etc. For you, it's a foundational belief and guiding principle in all aspects of your life that all human beings are created equal and should be treated with respect.

12. *Discrimination Between Ends and Means:* You see a clear differentiation between the ends and the means when examining issues and you don't agree that the ends necessarily justify the means. Instead, you believe that the journey is often even more valuable than the destination. Because of this, you take the time to consider what is right—not just what will make the most money—in each situation and you have strong ethical standards that guide your business decisions. Your ideas of wrong or evil are often not the same as the conventional ideas of right and wrong, and your ability to discriminate between the two requires less rigidity than those with more black and white beliefs of "good and bad."

13. *Non-Hostile Sense of Humor:* While you love humor and a good joke about yourself or the human condition in general, you are repelled by jokes made at the expense of others either through hostility, smut, or making others out to be inferior. For you, it just isn't funny if someone else gets hurt or victimized.

14. *Creativity:* You are highly creative, naturally able to see things in a fresh light and from new angles. You

easily produce original and inventive works and often feel the need to "create." You might regularly express your creativity in any number of ways, such as through writing a blog, speaking to groups, painting, handicrafts, or creating a new business or product.

15. *Resistance to Enculturation*: You have the ability to transcend the culture in which you find yourself, which allows you to maintain a strong sense of individuality and to evaluate your own culture in a more objective way than most. At the most basic level you are a non-conformist. You aren't influenced by social pressure to fit in; instead you make decisions based on what you sense is intrinsically best for you at any particular moment or under any given circumstances.

16. *Imperfections*: Even though you are generally comfortable with who you are, you still find yourself striving to reach your full potential. You aren't perfect—you suffer from the typical human failings and can certainly have emotional outbursts—but you know it, and you're okay with your own humanness. You actually enjoy discovering new shortcomings, because it gives you a new area to explore your boundaries and pursue growth.

17. *Resolution of Opposites*: You find it easy to transcend contradictions that others have difficulty resolving. Self-actualizers go beyond the dichotomy of selfish and unselfish because they can see these characteristics as two sides of one coin—they know that we can be at once both things expressed in different ways. You don't feel a

pressing need to see things in black or white or to choose sides, and you can hold seemingly disparate ideas in your head at once without feeling conflicted or confused.

Your Business is Your Vehicle

You may already identify strongly with some of the traits of the self-actualized, but what if you aren't exhibiting all of these characteristics yet? When we are stalled in our own development, we can feel depressed, bored, restless, angry, unmotivated, or like we just want to give up. When we start feeling these negative feelings, we often unknowingly get stuck in this negative place, unable to progress and blaming outside circumstances for our internal feelings. All the while, the part of us that knows there is a higher dimension of our own being is trying to push us along, quietly rooting for us in the background.

Not living up to your full potential, or failing to even try, doesn't mean that you lose the innate desire to self-actualize. It's instinctual; as humans we all have this desire. We can't escape it. The part of our being that seeks to rise and fulfill our own unique potential is literally depressed by the weight of living a life that doesn't allow its full expression. When we suppress our consciousness—when we turn ourselves "off" so to speak—we are often left with a haunting sense of something left undone, a feeling that something is incomplete in our lives. If we want to live in a more harmonious state in life and in our work, we have no choice but to allow this natural inclination toward personal evolution to move us forward.

So how exactly do we begin to do that without dropping everything and going to meditate in a cave somewhere? This book lays the groundwork for some of the core mindset shifts necessary to create a habit of consciousness that supports self-actualization. Unlike the multitude of self-help and self-improvement books out there, I'm not going to ask you to take time out of your business to do this work. Instead, I offer you a wholly new approach to the concept of personal growth that benefits your soul as much as it does your sanity and your wallet. I'm going to show you how you can use your business as the vehicle that will carry you on this journey.

Approaching your business this way will help you develop the traits you need to have the most fulfilling life possible. Not only will understanding these principles leave you feeling more satisfied, you'll also have the motivation, passion, and power you need to overcome any obstacles that your business faces – now, and in the future.

How to Use This Book

Through my experience as an entrepreneur, business coach, spiritual minister, intuitive healer, and meditation instructor, I've witnessed people struggle to put their finger on the yearning that pulls at them when they are unconscious of their deeper needs. This book follows the guidance I've shared with so many others about how to start shifting the way we engage with our lives in order to identify and fulfill our need to reach our highest potential.

I didn't write this book to tell you what to think or believe. In fact, please don't just believe everything I tell you! Instead, I simply invite you to use the tools offered here to investigate for yourself how these different perspectives feel and what opportunities they illuminate for you through your own experience.

You may have heard the now-famous story "This is Water," told by David Foster Wallace as part of his commencement speech for the Kenyon College class of 2005. The story begins, "There are these two young fish swimming along when they happen to meet an older fish swimming the other way who nods at them and says, 'Morning, boys, how's the water?' The two young fish swim on for a bit, and then eventually one of them looks over at the other and goes, 'What the hell is water?'" The point is simple: The most obvious, important realities are often the ones we take for granted, so much so that they're hard to see and even talk about. I want to help you see and be able to talk about the water you swim in each day. Perhaps even more importantly, I'm going to show you how to swim in that water with less stress, fewer obstacles, and more satisfaction.

Real, substantial, lasting change requires a willingness to move outside of what we *think* we know. Each chapter will present a core understanding that will expand your consciousness and is foundational to your ability to reach your highest potential. Each chapter also offers key exercises to help you integrate these concepts in a way that is practical and relevant to your own experience in life and business. As you read, keep in mind the self-evaluation you did on Maslow's traits of the self-actualized individual. Consider how you might grow by applying the methods and activities of each chapter.

A Word About Truth and Resistance

The concepts in this book aren't meant to be accepted as part of a belief system. Rather, as one of my spiritual teachers, Diego Palma, often says, "Ask for yourself: What is true?" The only way you can know whether something is true for you is to try it on for size and decide for yourself. This requires a certain amount of willingness to engage with discomfort and unfamiliarity in order to grow.

Your first lesson in consciousness begins now: Watch your own internal reactions with a great deal of curiosity as you read this book. If something doesn't ring true for you, before you simply discard it, I ask that you put it through an evaluation. There is a distinction to be made between "that doesn't sound right to me" and "that's stupid."

If something doesn't sound right to you, or if you feel like it isn't applicable to you, it may be because you haven't had that experience or that the concept is unfamiliar to you. In this case, instead of dismissing something outright, I ask you to "put it on the shelf for future enlightenment." This allows for openness to anything the idea holds of value for you and your journey when the time is right—sometimes an idea isn't true for you...until it is. And if the time is never right and it's never revealed, so be it.

Conversely, if you read something and have a huge negative reaction to it, this should be a sign to become even more curious. We often have very negative reactions to the things we most need to hear. When I teach yoga, I explain to my students that there are two different kinds of resistance. One is your body's innate wisdom alerting you to danger, such as the pain you might feel when you are about to pull a muscle or injure yourself. The other is your ego's mental defense against pushing past previously held ideas of what is possible for you, such as a running narrative in your mind about how hard it is to hold a certain position, or how much you hate a certain series of poses. If we are ever going to meet our true potential, we have to know which kind of resistance is which.

All change, even good change, brings a certain amount of discomfort. When reading this book, if you feel that something just isn't meant for you, move on. But if you feel internal resistance to something, stay with it. Shining a light on what's really motivating us is one important way that we expand our consciousness and stop our mind-driven ego from running us—and our businesses—into the ground. It's the needs we don't examine that end up driving us toward suffering. When you find something in this book that brings out a strong reaction of any kind, just pause and notice what's happening for you. Then, take some notes so that you can apply the techniques you will learn later in this book to further investigate your resistance.

Becoming a more conscious person is not an academic exercise. You must try it on for size one moment at a time. See what happens if you don't listen to the stories your mind is telling you about why an exercise or concept is stupid or won't help you. Having experiences in which your mind tells you something, and staying with the idea long enough to discover that the truth is the opposite, will give you an important benchmark. You'll look back on it the next time you face a false boundary and see the current resistance for what it is—the sign of another opportunity for you to learn and grow.

CHAPTER 1

Oneness

Thousands of years ago the gurus and sages of the East set out to determine the essential nature of reality. Through various means including meditation, fasting, scholarly studies of ancient philosophical texts, and renunciation, they devoted themselves to this quest with absolute determination. One of the key things they discovered was that all things are connected: What seems to be a multiplicity of things in the world is actually one thing manifesting in different forms. While this report came from their subjective spiritual exploration, the objective world of science has begun making startling discoveries about the universe that seem to coincide with these ancient teachings. It appears that there really is one "essence" connecting all of life—religious people may call it God, Brahman, or "great spirit" while modern-day physicists call it the Higgs Field. Put simply, at the most fundamental level the entire universe is connected by, and created from, an energy field that scientists have discovered exists everywhere.

Modern physics has determined that matter itself—and therefore every "thing" in the universe—is made up of energy vibrating at different frequencies. At the subatomic level, the particles that make up the atom are really constructed from tiny bits of vibrating energy gaining mass from the same shared field. Amazingly, this is the same conclusion that the ancient sages came to thousands of years ago: We are all a part of the same thing and separateness is simply an illusion. This illusion of separateness—of self and other, mind and body, inside and outside—pervades our awareness so deeply that it is nearly imperceptible to our minds, much like a fish in water.

This dualistic perception of reality is a paradox—it is both true and untrue simultaneously. Each of us has the experience of being an individual, separate part of existence, but at a deeper level we are all, both figuratively and literally, simply different parts of the same thing. For example, when you think of your parents, you think of beings separate from you. It seems as though you are not your mother or father. However, from the perspective of your DNA you are very much both your mother and your father. Consider that, while it appears that you are separate from this very book that you are holding, at the subatomic level you and the book are composed of the exact same things—protons, neutrons, electrons, and all of the various subatomic particles that construct them. Learning to live from the perspective of oneness means becoming comfortable with the paradoxical nature of reality, viewing the hard divisions we perceive between ourselves and our environment, and one another, with less rigidity.

This awareness of fundamental oneness is the home base for your journey to self-actualization. This way of perceiving reality is paramount; without this insight it is impossible for you to reach your full potential because you are not in alignment with the "house rules" of the universe. When you are able to view everything in your life from this perspective, it opens the door to a new and paradigm-shifting relationship with life itself. If everything in the universe is a part of you, then any of the various phenomena you encounter—people, relationships, and even your business—are capable of teaching you about yourself and assisting your personal growth.

However, as humans we have a perceptual bias to view things dualistically. It's one thing to talk about this way of perceiving existence—that all things are one—and it's a whole other thing to actually experience it for yourself and learn to live from that perspective. Unfortunately, reading these words won't end your habit of perceiving dualistically, but the critical first step in making any change is awareness. Building awareness of this perspective by remembering it as often as you can will help cement it in your consciousness and bring it into your everyday life. Think of this type of work much like building muscle—you need to work out consistently to see results. In this case, the workout is simply trying to remember more often than you forget.

Sometimes people hear the phrase "shifts in consciousness" and imagine this means some kind of Earth-shattering, woo-woo spiritual awakening. It definitely can be that, but most of the time a shift in consciousness simply means a new way of seeing, experiencing, or understanding reality. A shift in consciousness is, in other words, simply a change in perspective. For example, consider...

...that when you stand next to a plant and breathe, you are breathing in the oxygen that the plant is breathing out, and the plant is breathing in the carbon dioxide that you are breathing out.

...that the air around you is not empty space at all, but actually filled with particles of elements like oxygen, hydrogen, etc.

...that there is no space on Earth that is truly empty. When you move, you are swimming through atoms of the same stuff from which the universe formed.

Go ahead. Just try on this perspective, as foreign as it may be, and see how it shifts things for you. It would be impossible to simply believe in the existence of oneness when it's not your experience of life, but I do invite you to consider that an erroneous perception we collectively share is not necessarily objective truth. Inviting this perspective into your everyday experience creates the potential for radical changes in your life, because with it comes the ability to take responsibility for the quality of your inner landscape. From this perspective, you may not be directly responsible for whatever happens in your life, but you are responsible for your *reaction* to whatever happens.

You Are Your Business, Your Business Is You

When viewing life from the perspective that all is one and everything is connected, we begin to realize that a lot of the boundaries we imagine between things don't really exist. The key boundary we want to start dissolving for the purposes of this book is the imagined one between yourself and your business. This is what drives many of us to feel like we have to make a choice between our personal growth and our business' growth. When you start to dissolve that boundary, you see that your personal health *is* the health of your business and vice versa. Neglecting your personal health and happiness so you can focus on your business makes no sense in a world where all things are one. Many entrepreneurs talk about trying to find a "work-life balance," but what we are going to try to develop here is work-life *integration*.

From this perspective, it's clear that anything you do to elevate yourself will naturally elevate your business. For your business to fully realize its potential, *you* need to fully realize *your* potential. Because of this, anything that hinders your personal growth and gets in the way of you achieving your full potential will likewise hinder the growth of your business. What, you ask, gets in the way of our growth the most and holds us back from our true potential? Simply put, it is unconscious patterns of thought and behavior. These are the parts of ourselves that are so deeply engrained we can't even tell they exist, but they are beneath the surface creating messes in our lives, affecting our judgment, and damaging our relationships. Call them by any name you like—habits, conditioning, unconsciousness, personality flaws—your goal is to become aware of their presence in your life and then (hopefully) change them for the better.

I can't tell you how many people I have counseled over the years who have come to me and said they were completely stressed because their businesses were falling apart. Deeper investigation typically led me to uncover that when someone said their business was falling apart, it wasn't the only problem—in most cases, other aspects of their life were falling apart too.

Cesar Milan, famous "dog-whisperer" and television personality, talks about how he does not find humans that have dog problems; he finds dogs that have human problems. Well guess what? Most of the people I have counseled about their failing businesses aren't owners with business problems; they have businesses with owner problems. The owner's unconscious patterns of thought and behavior have created problems within their business, often the same problems they also have in their personal life.

One of my clients, whom we'll call Sam, owns a business that provides a prime example of this. With his permission, I'll share his story here because it perfectly illustrates this point. Sam is considered an industry leader in his sector, and Sam's business has hundreds of outstanding online reviews from satisfied customers. His business receives tons of referrals from other professionals in his field and has a stellar reputation for providing great service. From the outside, everything looked great, but the inside of Sam's business was completely broken. When I first started working with Sam, although his company was grossing nearly half a million dollars in revenue each year, he didn't keep books, he hadn't paid business taxes in years, he was paying people as subcontractors who were actually employees, and was not holding client funds in escrow. To say that it was a mess would be a vast understatement.

It was clear to me on paper that Sam's business was completely capable of making a substantial profit every year, and that the service it provided its clients was indeed top-notch. The issue was that Sam, as the owner, made decisions based on how he wanted his company to be perceived, not based on how it actually *was*. Money was spent frivolously to maintain the appearance of success and, although the business could easily have turned a healthy profit, it was instead a financial disaster because of his choices.

Ultimately, it turned out these problems were a perfect reflection of Sam's personal life. Through our work together, I discovered this pattern of self-deception and need to "keep up with the Joneses" was pervasive in every facet of his life. It appeared from the outside that he had a happy family, but his marriage was actually falling apart. On the outside he was buying new cars, but in reality he was rolling the unpaid balance from one car into the payment for the next car. On the outside he was successful and prosperous, but the truth was that Sam was deeply in debt. The list goes on and on. Many of the problems the business had were simply extensions of Sam's personal problems—because from the perspective of oneness there is no difference between the two. Sam was living a lie, and his business was too.

Were there tangible changes to be made to resolve the business problems? Of course—messes can always be cleaned up, but each mess was nothing more than a symptom of a much larger problem. The deeper and more important issue was that Sam was living in denial. He needed to learn how to come to grips with reality and make decisions based on recognition of the truth, rather than what he wished it to be or how he wanted it to be perceived by others. To acknowledge that you have been living a lie is not easy work, but it was essential work for Sam to actually fix the problems in his business and his life.

You, as a business owner, are the driver of the vehicle that is your business. If you aren't aware of the patterns within you that affect your driving, there's a high likelihood that you'll encounter problems along your journey. These patterns create "blind spots" for you and your business, because you aren't aware of their presence or the effects they're having. Becoming aware of your patterns and conditioning is absolutely critical to maximizing your potential as an entrepreneur, because those patterns will inevitably manifest themselves in everything you create—after all, your business is just an extension of you.

Mirror, Mirror

The easiest way to become aware of your mental and emotional patterns is, interestingly enough, the same way you would look at yourself physically—by using a mirror. Because these patterns are so deeply embedded in our subjective experience, it's actually easier to recognize them outside when they're reflected back to us. By using some specific tools and techniques, it's possible to see your patterns and learn to recognize them—that way, when you know they are running, you can then begin to make a different choice to break the pattern and its hold over you.

A great exercise to help us become more conscious of our patterns comes from one of my favorite authors, life coach Martha Beck, in which she describes an awesome technique that I use with all of my clients called "You Spot It, You Got It."

This is a modern technique for working with what Carl Jung, the father of analytical psychology, referred to as our "shadow." He noted that each of us has aspects of our personality that we are either ignorant of, or that we deny exist at all, and this is the shadow—the very unconsciousness we are working to uncover and bring awareness to. Everyone has a shadow, which is irrational and highly prone to *psychological projection*—a behavior in which a person will defend themselves against their own unpleasant impulses by attributing them to other people. For example, someone who is selfish will frequently accuse other people of being selfish, or someone who wastes resources will accuse someone else of being wasteful. This basically means that whatever we can't stand the most in others, not just the things we find mildly disagreeable but those things that really drive us crazy, are actually just our own traits being reflected back at us and even sometimes amplified. As Beck says, "To feel good about acting in ways that are reprehensible to ourselves, we must repress our recognition that we're doing so...we become hyper alert to anything that reminds us of the behavior we're denying in ourselves, focusing with unusual intensity on the slightest hint of that behavior in others, or imagining it where it doesn't even exist." Each of us has had the experience of seeing this happen for other people—the "pot calling the kettle black"—but our task is to turn this around and point our awareness at ourselves to see the ways in which we are doing this. By recognizing our reflections and projections, we are able to use the outside world as a mirror for our own unconsciousness.

There are two ways that I work with clients on this topic. The first is by using Martha Beck's "You Spot It, You Got It" exercise.[1]

---

[1] This exercise is an excerpt from the full article on Martha Beck's blog at: http://marthabeck.com/2012/01/projection-when-what-you-spot-is-what-youve-got/

Exercise: You Spot It, You Got It

1. Phase One: Write Your Rant

To begin, list all the nasty, judgmental thoughts you're already thinking about Certain People/Other Businesses. Who's offending you most right now? What do you hate most about them? What dreadful things have they done to you? What behavior should they change? Scribble down all your most controlling, accusatory, politically incorrect thoughts.

2. Phase Two: Change Places

Now go through your written rant and put yourself in the place of the person you're criticizing. Read through it again, and be honest—could it be that your enemy's shoe fits your own foot? If you wrote "Kristin always wants things her way," could "I always want things my way" be equally true? Could this be the very reason Kristin's selfishness bothers you so much? If you wrote "Joe has got to stop clinging and realize that our relationship is over," could it be that you are also hanging on to the relationship—say, by brooding all day about Joe's clinginess?

3. Sometimes you'll swear you don't see in yourself the loathsome qualities you notice in others. You spot it, but you ain't got it. Look again. See if you are implicitly condoning someone else's vileness by failing to oppose it—which puts your actions on the side of the trait you hate. You may be facilitating your boss's combativeness

by bowing your head and taking it, rather than speaking up or walking out. Maybe you hate a friend's greediness, all the while "virtuously" allowing her to grab more than her share. Indirectly you are serving the habits you despise. Your rant rewrite may look like this example from one of my clients, Lenore:

Phase One: The Rant

"My kids take me for granted. They expect me to drop whatever I'm doing and focus on them, anytime. I'm sick of them taking me for granted."

Phase Two: The Rewrite

"I take me for granted. I expect me to drop whatever I'm doing to focus on my kids, anytime. I'm sick of me taking me for granted."

Writing these scripts helps you get unstuck from a dualistic perspective because whenever you think the problem is about someone or something else, it reminds you that, no, it is really just about you and what you can do for yourself. Once you have the rewritten script, you have to apply the wisdom to make the change—and this means making a different choice and taking a different action than you otherwise would. Using the above example, for instance, if you discover that you are sick of taking yourself for granted, you have to make a plan for how you are going to start giving more energy and focus to yourself—and then actually do it.

Another tool I use to work with this "mirror principle" is a simple, powerful practice using the statement, "Just like me." Anytime I find myself having something negative to say about a client, team member, or a competitor I tack this phrase on the end as a reminder that, whether I see it in that moment or not, "you spot it, you got it" has always proven true. Reminding ourselves that we are all one, and that the speck in someone else's eye is the log in our own, also helps to cultivate compassion for others as well as ourselves.

Exercise: Just Like Me

If you can't see how you may be projecting in a certain situation it's usually not because you aren't, but rather that you just can't fully see it yet.

For example, you might think, "This other company spends way too much money on advertising, it's their own fault they make bad decisions and can't get in the black." Maybe you know that you definitely don't spend way too much money on advertising; in fact you couldn't even afford to put more money in your advertising budget this year.

In cases like this, I find that "you spot it, you got it" is operating more like a funhouse mirror—a slightly distorted view. Maybe you don't spend too much on advertising, but maybe you are wasting money or resources in some other way and aren't able to take an honest look at it. So you can simply add the reminder to a slightly adjusted version, such as, "This other company spends way too much money...*just like me.*"

Of course this same principle can also help us in a positive way, as many of us often have a great deal of difficulty accepting all of our many wonderful traits. The next time you find yourself thinking, "Wow, she is so generous and kind," also add a "just like me." This is a powerful way to support the characteristic of acceptance and human kinship.

Learning to recognize your reflections and projections is a great way to identify your blind spots and work to change them. Don't be afraid to make light of this practice, either, and make a joke if that works for you. When you are able to see the irony that the hard look into the mirror of life provides you will indeed get a good chuckle. Life is not without a wicked sense of humor.

The Way You Do One Thing is the Way You Do Everything

It took me years to fully understand what one of my spiritual teachers, Colette Chase, meant when she said, "The way you do one thing is the way you do everything." It's not always a complete picture, but you will often find that when you encounter a recurring problem in your business, that same energy pattern also exists in other aspects of your life. Because you're dealing with patterns of thought and behavior, those patterns will often manifest themselves at multiple levels simultaneously. The key is to be willing to ask yourself the hard questions. Once you can be honest about what is not working in your business, take an honest look as to whether that same thing is not working in other areas of your life. This works the opposite way as well. If something isn't working in your personal life, take the time to investigate how that might be reflected in your business. You might be surprised at what you find. Turn this into a regular practice and you may become adept at uncovering problems before they explode into crises, both personally and professionally.

Once you've become someone who really understands that the way you do one thing is the way you do everything, and when you really understand that all is one, you start interacting with your environment in a very different way. It doesn't take as long for you to reap the benefits of your errors when you aren't wasting time blaming others. Your learning curve gets much shorter and you grow through the growing pains of your business much faster, because *you* aren't getting in the way as much. Imagine how much just this shift alone would help you in moving toward your business goals. By choosing to see any challenges and setbacks you encounter as an opportunity for growth and development, you will also have a better attitude and be much more resilient in the face of adversity.

The truth is that you will always face obstacles in your life and in your business. By approaching your role as an entrepreneur from the perspective of oneness, you give yourself the tools to turn those obstacles into opportunities to self-actualize and heal, instead of remaining trapped in a cycle of frustration and suffering.

Exercise: How's *That* Working for You?

List three things that are working really well in your business (e.g. we are in the black, we have a supportive team of employees/contractors, etc.)

1._____

2._____

3._____

Now look at these three things and ask yourself, are the correlates of these things in my personal life also true? (e.g. You're not in serious debt and are running your personal finances in the black; you have a supportive group of friends and family.) If not, go back and ask yourself, are things really running as well as I think they are? At this point there is nothing "to do" about these things. Just notice them, for better or worse— remember, awareness is the first step to changing behavior. For now, focus on being willing to see things as they really are.

Now list three things that are not going well in your business.

1._____

2._____

3._____

Ask yourself, are the same areas also suffering in my personal life? There may not be a direct, obvious correlation, so it's important to remember the funhouse mirror analogy. Problems may not be an exact reflection; instead you are looking for similar patterns. For example, if you can't seem to get rid of the old inventory in your warehouse, you might ask yourself, "What in my personal life am I also struggling to get rid of, and why?"

Now, for each item above, list its corresponding personal issue:

1._____

2._____

3._____

Once you are aware of these issues in your business and your personal life you can start to apply the advice that American theologian, Reinhold Niebuhr, espoused in his famous "Serenity Prayer." Try it as a personal mantra (substitute whatever word for God you wish): "God grant me the serenity to accept the things I cannot change, the courage to change the things I can, and the wisdom to know the difference." Ask yourself what changes you can make today to start truly fixing those problems that you have the ability to change.

No Victims Here!
(The Belief that Keeps You Stuck)

As we begin to move into a sustained awareness of oneness and more personal responsibility for the quality of our inner landscape, we find that there are certain patterns or attitudes that are simply incompatible with this new worldview. One of them—not surprisingly—is victimhood. Victimhood is, by its very definition, incompatible with personal responsibility because being a victim requires placing blame on something outside ourselves. True, we may not be able to control the circumstances of our lives, but taking responsibility for our reaction to those circumstances means ending these dualistic tendencies—self and other, good and bad, praise and blame—and moving into a more holistic approach.

When we perceive our world from a dualistic point of view there is an inherent tension. Feel into that for yourself—can you sense the tension between "us and them," "mine and yours," "for and against?" When we perceive ourselves as a small, isolated "self" that is disconnected from the rest of life we tend to have tremendous fear and anxiety. Life feels like a struggle all the time, and it's a constant fight between our sense of self and the world "out there."

Often when we encounter problems, we subconsciously believe that the source of these problems is external, especially in business. It's a common reaction to look at our business challenges from the dualistic perspective of competition: self vs. other, victim vs. perpetrator. This is the reason that so many of our business analogies in the West are sports or warfare metaphors—part of our culture involves the need for there to be a protagonist and an antagonist. When you aren't looking at the world through the lens of "oneness," the default is often to see yourself as the victim. You're the victim of changing circumstances in your business, a failing economy, a bad employee who let you down, a lousy partner who betrayed you. You don't have to take responsibility because someone or something outside of you is to blame.

Living from a state of victimhood means making yourself completely powerless to outside forces. When you are a victim, you put yourself, and your business, in a position to be pushed by the winds of change without any influence on the outcome. Living in this victim state also comes with a host of other problems including paranoia, indecisiveness, and a tendency to make only incremental changes instead of taking bold action. This isn't to say that you should blame yourself for all of the negative circumstances of your life—far from it—we are trying to overcome the impulse to engage in blame in the first place.

Blame is a very toxic energy that does nothing except keep us stuck. When we push out our internal upset onto others, or even turn it on ourselves, we then make it impossible to actually deal with our own feelings about whatever situation we may find ourselves in. Instead we are left with unresolved feelings that we are now expecting someone else to be responsible for. Do you see how little sense it makes to put our own healing and resolution in the hands of someone else? By blaming others, we can never acknowledge the parts of the situation we may have contributed to and need to take responsibility for, thus leaving us vulnerable to creating the same pattern, in varying forms, over and over again.

What does all this have to do with dualism and oneness? Well, in order for us to believe that someone else is to blame for our upset, we first have to believe they are separate from us—in other words, we have to identify them as an outside cause for our internal state of anxiety

and fear. If we could see there is no true distinction between us and the other person, we would not seek to
push our negative feelings outside of us and onto them.
When all things are one, we understand that the problem
isn't just out there, it's also in here. There is no meaningful difference, which means blame is ultimately pointless.
We don't shift into blaming ourselves instead of others,
either, for the same reason. Instead, we recognize that by
changing our internal reality, we can affect change in our
external reality, which gives us back our power over our
own healing and resolution, and our control over recre-
ating situations that have caused us upset in the past.

It's All *for* You

In addition to enabling a greater degree of clarity and
responsibility in our lives, maintaining awareness of the
interconnectedness of all things also gives us an empow-
ering new perspective to work from. Because we are
each, as individuals, inextricably linked to anything and
everything in the universe, we can choose to adopt a
mindset that everything—seriously, *everything*—that happens in our lives and our businesses happens for our
benefit. Even situations which seem terrible carry with
them the possibility of helping us grow.

People who completely resist the idea of oneness sys-
tematically give up their power and control over their
own state of being. Their lives, and therefore their businesses, become one big reflection of their mental and

emotional patterns. They cultivate tension through a dualistic perception of reality, thus priming themselves for upset, and they fail to learn from their experiences. Because they are too busy blaming their external circumstances instead of taking the opportunity for reflection; they don't make the necessary changes and instead keep creating the same results. People operating from this space also start to emphasize the "unfairness" of the world or their "bad luck" in their minds. This is a surefire way to destroy your motivation, because this kind of thinking saps the strength and energy you could be using to put toward your goals.

But, when you start to view things from the perspective that everything is connected, then you realize that in every moment you have the power to make a new choice. If the problem isn't entirely "out there," then you have some degree of control over the conditions that created it, and you can therefore avoid creating it in the future. From this perspective, you are not living at the whim of the universe or ill-meaning people. Even in situations where you truly have little control over the circumstances, you recognize that you *always* have control over your internal state and the way you respond to the world. Once you shift your perspective out of the victim mindset you begin to see that in reality, things are not happening *to* you but they are happening *for* you.

All of the circumstances you encounter are an opportunity for you to grow and develop strength and wisdom, whether you view it as God challenging you, the work of a benevolent energetic Universe, or simply a pragmatic approach of accepting things as they truly are. No matter what happens, no matter how good or how devastating, from the perspective of oneness you can reclaim the choice to look at your situation as if it's happening *for you*, presenting you with an opportunity to take one step closer to the fulfillment of your highest potential.

This one shift puts you in a much more powerful place where you are the responsible party at the center of your life. You can actually make a choice to make a difference. When you live this way, you and your business will thrive, because you are steering the ship instead of being pushed by the winds of change. Reaching our highest potential cannot happen without being fully responsible for ourselves.

Noticing Our "Preferences"

There is an old Zen story about a farmer who had a horse that broke through his fence and ran away. When his neighbors heard what happened, they came to the farmer and said, "Oh no! What terrible luck! How awful that you now don't have a mare during planting season." The farmer listened and then replied, "Bad luck, good luck—who knows?"

A few days later, the horse returned to the farm with two stallions. When the neighbors heard, they visited the farmer. "What great fortune this is! You are now going to be a very rich man," they said. The farmer listened and again replied, "Good luck, bad luck—who knows?"

Soon after, the farmer's only son was thrown from one of the new horses and broke his leg. When the neighbors learned of this, they came to the farmer. "It is planting season and now that your son has a broken leg, there is no one to help you," they said. "This is truly bad luck." The farmer listened, and once more he said, "Bad luck, good luck—who knows?"

The next day, the emperor's army rode into the town and drafted the eldest son from every family to fight in the war. The only son not taken, because of his broken leg, was the farmer's. Soon the neighbors returned. They said, "Yours is the only son who was not taken from his family and sent to war. What good luck this is..."

"Good luck, bad luck—who knows?" The point of the parable is to illustrate that our views of good and bad, attraction and aversion are all relative. Holding tightly to a specific belief of how the world should be, when the reality is that we have no clue what the "best" outcome is, only creates suffering.

The social media marketing revolution is a great example of how the concretization of preferences works. Even now that social media has become an integral part of how we all buy, sell, and communicate, you can probably think of one or two of your colleagues who've expressed a resistance to learning these tools or using them to reach their target audience. I know I have heard this type of resistance from many, many entrepreneurs. In the wedding industry, for example, the average age at the time of first marriage is presently twenty-eight years old. It's no surprise that social media is a major source of buying influence for young couples. And yet, I still meet many business owners in the wedding industry who don't have Facebook pages, don't use Twitter, and don't want to bother with Instagram or any other social media platform.

When a coaching client recently complained about a decline in new leads for her business over the last ten years, I asked about her social media strategy. She told me it was too hard to keep up with the changing options and that what she did in the past (print advertising) had always worked, so she was still focusing on that. I explained that while she had gotten older, the average age of her customer had stayed relatively the same. The clients she was trying to court were online, and she wasn't. The problem, and its solution, seemed fairly obvious.

Her response? "What I did before always worked well, so I really think I just need to do that again, but maybe learn to do it better. Plus, I *hate* social media."

Her concretized belief of what works for her business, mixed with her aversion to social media, created a situation where she was stuck. Staying stuck in this case meant that her business kept declining year after year, and she needed to find a way out of this conundrum. In order to assist her, I taught her how to use a heightened awareness of her own aversions and attractions as a way to stay open and begin to move her business forward.

An essential part of the perspective of a self-actualized person involves the ability to resolve apparent dichotomies and become comfortable with paradox. After all, there is no need to relate to things in terms of their opposites when you realize that they are nothing more than different sides of the same coin. Moreover, releasing our need to view things dualistically helps us accept the fact that pleasing and difficult circumstances in life will constantly alternate. Many people who are not doing the work of self-actualization see it as totally normal to look at opposites like pleasure and pain, praise and blame, loss and gain, and to try to constantly align with the "positive" side of the equation. After all, who wouldn't rather experience praise over blame?

Becoming more conscious involves understanding that suffering comes not only from experiencing pain, but from struggling to experience *only* pleasure. This resistance to experiencing pain or disappointment is itself a source of suffering, often much more than whatever pain we might be trying to avoid. Constant pleasure is no more an ordinary state of life than constant pain. Life includes both sides of the coin, it always has and it always will. The only way to break down these concretized beliefs that we mistakenly think will help us stay happy and avoid suffering is to become aware of them. We want to be conscious of the moment when we're about to make a decision based on an unconscious preference for avoiding discomfort, so we can make better, clearer choices for ourselves and our businesses.

The following exercise, practiced over and over again, will begin to break down these concretized walls that govern the way you experience your reality. I recommend doing this activity once a month, or anytime you find yourself feeling stuck on an issue and unable to move forward.

Exercise: Attraction or Aversion

It is not enough to just read this exercise—you must try it on for yourself to experience its true power. First, read through these instructions thoroughly, then get up and do it!

Get up and go for a five minute walk – around your office, the block, or the house. You are going to move around with an attitude of curiosity. Try and reside in the place of your mind that is just witnessing your own thoughts. Let your eyes scan your surroundings and allow yourself to become aware of all of the many subtle ways that you are "for" or "against" something. For example, you might take a walk through your office and see a plaque for an award you won, and your thoughts might go something like, "Mmm, yes, I like that, that was a good day when I won that award. People really took notice after that." This would be an example of attraction to what you experienced.

Then you might look down and notice that someone has spilled coffee on the rug and your thoughts might sound something like, "Ugh, that looks so dirty. That is not how I want my clients to think we keep this office." This is an example of aversion to what you experienced.

While you are in the five minute experiment, and after for that matter, don't judge your experience. Just see what you feel and think. This is about increasing your awareness of concretized, "pain vs. pleasure" thinking and practicing your acceptance of these imperfections. It's okay to laugh at yourself, by the way. It can be comical when you realize how many things you have a concretized "for" and "against" feeling that you weren't even aware of.

When you're done with your five minutes, come back and write down five things you were attracted to:

1._____

2._____

3._____

4._____

5._____

Now, write down five things you felt an aversion to:

1._____

2._____

3._____

4._____

5._____

Don't try to change your attraction or aversion to things. Just relax into the realization that this is how things are for you, and notice that this is happening *all the time*. Don't try to resist it; resistance is suffering! The way to really apply the power of your conscious awareness on this is to simply observe your inner landscape with as much kindness, compassion, and honesty as possible. When we are aware of this tendency within ourselves for attraction and aversion, we tend to take it much less seriously—which leads to less suffering. Taking this perspective also helps prevent us from getting "locked on" to a specific preference, instead maintaining a fresh openness to many different possibilities. The result is better decisions, less resistance, and more peace and clarity.

Finding Our Way

In order to fulfill your greatest potential as an entrepreneur, you have to be able to take an honest appraisal of how things are *right now*. By using the tools in this chapter, you have removed some of the key blocks that keep you from seeing clearly. Continued work in this area will further your understanding and acceptance of the concept of oneness, so that you can begin to resolve issues at a root level rather than just temporarily solving them on the surface.

Approaching your life, and your business, from the perspective of oneness will reap tangible benefits for you personally and professionally, because maintaining a wider perspective always produces better results. As each of us progresses in this type of work, it's important to cultivate a healthy appreciation for paradox, rather than viewing things as black-and-white, this-or-that. Often, the choices that seem so clear from one perspective are quite a bit muddier than we initially assume.

Realizing this, how can we bring the perspective of oneness and connection into our everyday experience? The answer is profoundly simple – the most important thing you can possibly do to support your growing awareness of oneness, and everything else we'll discuss in this book, is to *be present*.

CHAPTER 2

Presence

Once we've begun to cultivate an awareness of the reality of the universe—that all things are one—our next step is learning to find a mental and emotional space where we can rest comfortably as we embrace all the new experiences awareness will bring. Whether you realize it or not, every new experience you encounter has the potential to alter your internal landscape and influence your ability to use the tools you'll learn in this book for greater consciousness and happiness. The space through which all experiences flow, the place we must learn to enter and stay in as much as possible so that we can process these new experiences productively, is the *present moment*.

For most of us, understanding what it truly means to be present is challenging because we have spent a lifetime being conditioned to do everything *but* be present. Our minds habitually wander out of the present moment, constantly narrating our experience while dwelling on the past or worrying about the future. All of us have a tendency to automatically leave the immediacy of our felt experience and follow the streams of these stories in our mind. Western culture has actually trained us to look forward to the future and learn from the past as a way of protecting ourselves—or so we think—against future problems and hurts.

By learning how to be present, we build the capacity to be flexible and move with the changing tides without undoing the steps we've taken toward self-actualization. In this chapter we will take a look at what value there is to "training in the now" and in what ways we habitually shut down to the present. By learning why we escape the present moment, and how to come back, you will be embarking on the deepest work—the training that lays the groundwork for self-actualization.

The Container of Now

Think of the present moment—*the now*—as a container that holds the space for your experience. If we strengthen, widen, and deepen our own container, we are able to more effectively deal with all of the myriad things both pleasant and unpleasant that inevitably arise within it. Working on our ability to become, and stay, present in any circumstance builds your container's *capacity* to handle anything which comes your way. The stronger you make your container of present moment awareness, the more successful you will be at maintaining peace, stability, and balance in your life despite an ever-changing environment.

The benefits of being present, also referred to in many circles as "mindfulness," in the workplace are many. Studies have shown that mindfulness training improves memory and reduces stress, which leads to less interpersonal conflict and stronger connections between co-workers, better customer service, and a number of other secondary benefits. When you are present, you are also more likely to notice problems and less likely to make mistakes.

I remember one time in particular when I was not staying present during a counseling session with one of my wedding clients. I had just learned that I was pregnant and I'd be having a baby in about eight months, which was great—but unexpected—news. I would normally have rescheduled our session, but I was so scattered that day I'd forgotten to reach out, and then suddenly my client was at my door. She spent the first part of our meeting talking about her life and telling stories about her family. Because I was in listening mode, it was easy for my mind to slip out of the present and into the future, especially given the big news I had just learned about my own life.

You can imagine the kinds of things running through my head that pulled at my attention far more than the stories my client was telling me, one of which was about her brother passing a few years before. I was so distracted that I missed this crucial detail. I completely put my foot in my mouth when I asked, "So for the ceremony, would you like to include a moment of silence? Is there anyone in your immediate family that has passed away recently?"

My client looked at me with disbelief. "Yes, my brother, remember?" she said.

I was mortified.

Staying present is especially important for those of us who are in a service-based business or interact with people on a regular basis, because it strengthens your ability to connect to others and really listen. We all have a deep need to feel heard and acknowledged—it's one of the many reasons why people go to, and benefit from, psychotherapy. However, if you are focused on the past or the future instead of listening to what someone is saying in the present moment, you miss important details, and the other person—like my poor client on that unfortunate day—won't feel heard at all.

This is It, Don't Miss It

Think back to when you first started your business and really bring that time of your life to your mind. What kinds of things were you worried about? What kind of hopes did you have for your new venture? I'm sure there were a great many concerns, hopes, and dreams that were running through your mind at the time. How many of the things you worried or dreamed about *actually* happened?

For business owners in particular, we focus much of our time on the future. We feel that our success lies in what we are able to achieve in the future, and spend a significant amount of time developing plans and strategies. We tend to think in terms like, "When my business does 1 million dollars in sales, *then* it will be a success." Maybe financially that will be true, but will you actually feel that way when the day comes? It's far more likely that instead you will be thinking about your next goal of two million. Why? Because when you focus on the future, you stay focused on the future, and you are never actually living in your present experience.

It's totally natural to want to move toward goals, and we will talk a lot about goals and taking action later in this book. However, your life never actually occurs in the past or the future—it only happens in the present moment. The past is already over, and any goals you make or strategies you devise point toward an imagined future that may or may not ever happen. In this way, the future and the past are actually completely illusory. They don't exist as states of time, only mental projections. Think about it. Where does the future exist? Where does the past exist? All we ever have is our experience right here in this very moment.

As anyone who has experienced the sudden loss of a loved one will tell you, it's important to cherish every moment because you never know when that person will be gone. It's wisdom we've all been taught: "Life is precious, savor every moment." But how many of us actually do this? The truth is that even when we have wonderful experiences that we want to savor and cherish, this habituation to "leave" the present moment still pulls on us.

Recently, I was speaking with some of the staff members at WeddingWire about doing a presentation for their annual conference. I deeply wanted to be chosen to speak in some capacity for the event, but I had submitted my application late and been told that the speaker slate was full and that it would likely take another year. I was disappointed, but grateful to have even been considered, so I let them know that if anything changed I would be ready at the drop of a hat. Just a few weeks before the conference, I got an email asking me to fill a panel spot that had just opened up. I was elated! I think I literally jumped out of my desk chair and did a happy dance. I was fully present with the joy I was feeling in that moment.

I have learned over the years that each moment is fleeting, so I tried to really savor the excitement. Within just a few minutes, though, I realized my thoughts were already trying to drag me into the future—what to say, what to wear, who would be there, and so on. I took notice of the stream of thoughts in my mind and I sat down, took a deep breath, and really tried to bring myself back to enjoying the moment—which now included a chuckle about how, no matter how much you practice these techniques, the habitual tendency of moving away into the future remains strong. I constantly remind myself, "This is it. Don't miss it." There is no moment outside of this one, and whether this moment presenting itself is pleasant or unpleasant, it's here for you to use as fuel for your self-actualization. Making a commitment to staying present means being willing to stay with the experience at hand, regardless of how it feels.

The techniques in this chapter, and throughout this book for that matter, are meant to help you be more present and aware in your life. Don't be discouraged if you aren't present all the time—that is not the goal and it's practically impossible. For our purposes, consider that your true goal is simply to *remember to be present more often than you forget.* Try my mantra on for size and remind yourself throughout your day, "This is it. Don't miss it."

In Zen Buddhism there is a saying, "Chop Wood, Carry Water." This instruction means that when you are doing the tasks that lead to your future (when you need wood for a fire or water to drink), you should stay immersed in the present task. So when you are chopping wood, chop wood. Don't be focused on carrying water, because it's not what is right now. When you are sitting in front of a customer in your office, really be present with them, as opposed to thinking about the last client that came in or the meeting you need to attend an hour later. The point of this instruction is to encourage you to give yourself over fully to every experience in the present moment and give it your full and undivided attention.

It seems like such obvious, simple advice, yet it's much easier said than done. If the now is always right here and the only "real" moment we have, then how is it so easy to keep getting lost in the past and future?

How We Go Missing

Have you ever had the experience of having a conversation with someone where everything seems to be going well, with both of you engaged in the conversation, and then all of a sudden something strange happens? You are in the middle of speaking when you notice that the expression on the other person's face has completely changed; it's like they have gone missing. Now your mind starts to race. "Was it something I said? Clearly it was, there is no one else here and nothing else going on. What was it? Are they upset with me?" You've definitely noticed that they have been emotionally affected and have now checked out of your conversation. I'm sure you have also been on the other end of this as well, perhaps realizing a few minutes into a conversation that you have no idea what the other person just said because you were too busy thinking about something else.

The opposite of presence is absence, and these types of scenarios occur when we leave the present moment and enter a stream of thinking about the past or future, or maybe even both—we go absent from our present experience. Because of our existing patterns, we view the present moment, and our future, through the lens of our past experience. If our past experiences include emotional pain, hearing or experiencing something that reminds us of this past experience triggers that emotional memory and brings it to the forefront of our awareness. Likewise, that same past experience can trigger a fear or worry about the future that feels as immediate as if it were happening right now. Either way, whenever this happens we are unintentionally polluting the present moment with meaning it doesn't actually have.

There are many different terms for this phenomenon, such as "being triggered," "getting hooked," or "having your buttons pushed." All of these phrases describe the nature of what is happening inside of us at the moment we go absent from our present experience. One of my favorite Buddhist teachers, Pema Chödrön, is known for describing this phenomena using the Tibetan word, *shenpa*. Shenpa literally translates to "attachment," meaning that there is an emotional attachment that pulls you out of the present moment and into the past or future. To me, the term shenpa encompasses the whole conglomeration of how we acquire emotional attachments, what we're attached to, and the process that involves that feeling of being pulled out of the moment by that attachment. Shenpa is an experience that's happening, not just a word that means you're attached to something and need to let go of it. It's an experience that all of us have, and recognizing it in yourself and others is crucial to coming back to presence.

I was recently talking to a florist who had spent a week designing and creating a large flower arrangement for a wedding. Her clients were very specific about their desires, and did not have a limit to their budget. Carol, the florist, was thrilled because she knew she could exercise her gifts to the fullest for the first time in her career. The day her clients were scheduled to arrive in the studio for a viewing and approval, a colleague walked in on the completed arrangement and exclaimed, "Whoa, that's um...pink!"

Carol told me her chest immediately tightened and feelings of insecurity arose. This would be the most expensive arrangement she had ever sold, and she feared she wasn't as good as "those" designers, the high-profile vendors who specialize in massive and expensive arrangements like she was trying to create. Her feelings of excitement and anticipation were immediately overtaken by her insecurity, which then turned into anger and blame. Carol blurted out, "Why in the hell did you wait till now to say something? If you hated it so much you could have said something when I showed you the design instead of letting me embarrass myself."

As you can imagine, her co-worker was taken aback. "I never said I hated it! You told me she wanted pink, Carol. This is pink, that's all I was saying."

This scenario happens, all the time, in a thousand different ways—and this, my friends, is shenpa. This is how we get "hooked." Something in our environment triggers a reaction to an emotional memory—in Carol's case, underlying insecurity—and it completely overwhelms the reality of the present moment. But once we are triggered and become absent, how do we come back to the present? How do we handle shenpa when it happens, and is there any way to prevent it from happening in the first place?

It's Never Too Late for Now

Had Carol fired her colleague for insulting her floral arrangement, it wouldn't have helped the uncomfortable feelings she was experiencing. If she had run away crying and wallowed in her feelings of shame and rejection, it wouldn't have helped either. The truth is that you can rarely, if ever, solve your internal discomfort by changing your external circumstances. Even if you manage to do so temporarily, emotional triggering is based on your underlying wounds and patterns and will only resurface in different situations later.

Instead, the moments where you find yourself triggered into an emotional reaction is the time to remind yourself, as Pema Chödrön says, "to *stay.*" Just stay with whatever unpleasant sensations or thoughts are arising inside of you—don't seek to do anything about them. Instead, meet shenpa with an attitude of curiosity. Take a pause, breathe, notice that you have been triggered, and then instead of beating yourself up about it or lashing out on someone else, take it inside. Stay with the feeling, no matter how uncomfortable it might be. As I always remind my coaching clients, *the only way out is through.*

The truth is that you can't stop shenpa, or even avoid it—it's part of our life experience. You can, however, shift *how* you experience it and your reaction to it. Instead of getting hooked by the story that it brings up from your past hurts or future fears ("I can't design flowers," "I will never be a seven-figure floral designer," "The bride is going to hate this") drop the story you are telling yourself and just stay present with any physical sensations that arise. For example, when you are effectively dealing with shenpa, you might say, "This feels like tightness in the chest, clenching in the jaw, heat in the cheeks." Doing this helps you bring those feelings into the container of the present moment, where you have the capacity to deal with them, and keeps your mind from pulling you off into a downward spiral of destructive thinking.

This type of inner work is what mindfulness training is meant for. When these triggering, shenpa-inducing moments occur, you can see them clearly for what they are and not get attached to the story of the chattering mind. When we are present, there is more space between our experience and our reaction to that experience, and that space allows for us to reflect on what is happening for us internally. If Carol could have been present and her container of the now was strong she would not have reacted to her colleague's remark so strongly. Instead of snapping, she could have excused herself and taken a moment alone to examine what it was about her coworker's comment that was so upsetting. She could have uncovered her underlying negative beliefs about herself and her work and learned that these beliefs still controlled her. In this way, the moment would have given her a great opportunity to bring more awareness to her old story of insecurity and to grow from it. With all of this raised awareness, Carol could have "reality tested" her insecurity by asking her coworker, "What did you mean by that?" or "I took that in a way that you may not have intended so can you clarify for me what you're saying?" When her coworker explained herself, Carol could have seen the gap between her perception and reality—another critical lesson for Carol on the road to self-actualization.

Exercise: The "Four R's"

I once had the pleasure of hearing a talk by Pema Chödrön in which she explained a four step process to use when we experience shenpa. I've interpreted it from my own perspective here. The way it works is simple: When you find yourself triggered, just remember the four R's!

1. *Recognize*: First, simply recognize the fact that you have been triggered. Want a great way to practice being triggered? Go spend a weekend with your parents. I've come to find our parents installed many of the buttons we have, and they know just how to push them. So, when you go to their house and your father asks you, "Why aren't you retired yet? Shouldn't your business be more successful by now?" you can *recognize* you are triggered and move onto the second R.

2. *Refrain*: While you may want to either choke your dad or run into your childhood bedroom and cry, just *refrain*. You've been down this road before, and you know where it leads. This time, choose to let go of the insecurities, fears, past disappointments, and other

negative feelings the trigger has brought into the present moment and refrain from taking any actions that would proliferate that storyline. This lack of reaction allows those underlying feelings that were triggered to rise up in your body instead. Please note that this will likely *increase* the intensity of the experience, not decrease it.

3 *Relax*: Do your best to *relax* into whatever feelings have arisen and be present with them. Simply meet your pain with relaxed awareness, rather than needing to move away from it or do something about it. In my personal practice, I imagine my exhalations are breathing air into a balloon inside of me, and that the balloon is creating more space for me to simply relax. Just as it would be difficult to relax in a tiny room with a poisonous spider, you might find it slightly easier to relax if you and that spider were in a football stadium instead. Create that internal space through your breath (which we will talk about more in a bit) and get present—this is the moment for you to tap into the capacity of the present. This practice reduces the level of emotional pressure, so you don't feel as compelled to immediate action—in relaxed space you can see things more clearly and with a wider perspective. Eventually, the pressure will dissipate and you can move on.

4. *Resolve*: It would be great if this meant resolving your emotional wounds so you never get triggered again, but it doesn't. Instead, you need to realize and accept that there really is no way to stop it from happening again

and again—you can only decrease the effect it has on you by being present with your emotions when they arise. You must *resolve* to continue this practice in all areas of your life *for the rest of your life*. The fourth and final R is about remembering more often than you forget—there is no "done" and we must instead do our best to meet these tender places within ourselves with compassion and patience.

Through doing this work over and over again, we begin to remove arrogance and soften our hard edges. We may not be able to stop getting triggered, but we can lower our reactivity to emotional upset by turning our attention inward and feeling our way through whatever arises within us. In business, just like in life, there will always be issues. Practicing the four R's when faced with shenpa helps reduce our own suffering, and helps keep us from creating more suffering in the world around us.

Creating the Space for Mindfulness

So far, we've discussed the importance of being more mindful and aware of your thoughts and emotions when you are triggered, but there are ways to bring this same mindful attention to the totality of your work day, not just when you are about to rip off someone's head or burst out in tears. By practicing habits of mindfulness and employing strategies to cultivate more presence in our lives, we can strengthen our container and build additional capacity for happiness, love, and joy as well.

Growth doesn't just happen in a mountaintop monastery or at a retreat. The point of this book is to show you how to incorporate the principles of conscious living into where you're already spending your time—at work, at home, and everywhere else life takes you. When you're infusing your everyday experience with present-moment awareness, you're able to connect with what you're doing more deeply and get better results, no matter what it is that you are doing or where you are.

One way to cultivate more presence in your day is by regularly taking a *sacred pause*—a small break to remind yourself to breathe and return to the present moment. We've already discussed taking a pause when you feel triggered, but stopping to take a sacred pause throughout your day helps to build present-moment awareness as your default experience in life.

I have two favorite techniques for reminding myself to return to the present moment, but any mnemonic device that will remind you multiple times per day will work. My first technique is that I use bathrooms and doorways as "entry points to the now." Every time I walk through a doorway or enter the bathroom, I have trained myself to take a sacred pause. There is nothing particularly significant about bathrooms or doorways, other than that I consistently encounter both throughout my day no matter where I am. I've been doing this for so long that I no longer even think about it or need to stop walking—I just return to my breath and connect with the ever-present now.

The other technique I use is a mindfulness bell app on my smartphone—there are a number of these available but my personal favorites are *Mindfulness Bell* and *Insight Timer*. Mindfulness Bell allows you to set a bell to ring at pre-determined intervals—I have mine set to go off once an hour. No matter where I am, whether it's in a meeting with clients or working at my desk, the bell reminds me to take a breath and to connect with my body as the gateway to my present experience. I've been doing this work for most of my life, but I still need that reminder. No matter how far along the path of self-actualization you are, you're never going to be in a state of perfect enlightenment all the time. We're all constantly struggling against a state of forgetfulness; it's just part of being human. Creating room for sacred pauses and using tools like these help you remember to be present for your life more often than you forget.

Exercise: Choose Your Sacred Pauses

Pick one thing that you will designate as a signal for you to stop your stream of thinking and take a sacred pause, returning to the present moment.

My sacred pause reminder is:

_____

Now try it. Activate your reminder, take a deep breath, close your eyes, bring awareness into the inner body and ask yourself, "How is it right now?"

Approach the answer to this question with compassion or, as one of my favorite meditation teachers, Tara Brach, says, "Approach your inner being as if you were approaching a small animal in the woods." If you came upon a cute, furry animal in the forest, you would approach it with friendliness, gentleness, and tenderness, right? Offer that same reception to the small whispering voice of your heart when you ask, "How is it right now?"

Let the answer to your inquiry be brought into that space of tenderness. In that way, you don't have to "like" what is happening inside of you—after all, it may be very unpleasant. Instead, you are just saying "Yes, I see you there, and I want to get closer to you. I want to experience you more fully." You don't have to think, "Oh goodie, fear! My favorite!" Instead, just say, "Yes, fear, I see you and you are welcome here."

Meditation and Mindfulness—The "Secret" Success Formula

The beauty of sacred pauses is that they can be done anytime and anywhere. That said, there is also a great benefit to establishing set times during your day to create this space for yourself. Habits deliver results—it's a fact. Making a habit of taking sacred pauses trains us to re-enter the body and re-direct our energy inward throughout the day, but establishing a regular meditation practice builds our capacity for presence, and fills our reserves for when we need them most. I recommend that every one of my clients begin a ten minute meditation practice every morning and every evening as a way of strengthening and deepening their connection to the present moment.

Many of the world's top business leaders tout meditation as part of their recipe for success. In a conversation at the John Main Centre for Meditation and Inter-Religious Dialogue at Georgetown University, Ray Dalio, billionaire founder of the world's largest hedge fund firm, said, "Meditation, more than anything in my life, was the biggest ingredient of whatever success I've had." Oprah Winfrey (CEO of Harpo Productions), Russell Simmons (Hip-hop mogul and founder of Global Grind), and Arianna Huffington (President and Editor-in-Chief at Huffington Post) all practice daily meditation and credit their practice with bringing them results personally and professionally. I encourage you to strongly consider establishing a daily meditation practice; in my opinion there is no better way to spend time on the path of personal growth than this.

There are plenty of online resources for guided meditation, including the excellent, free recorded talks from the Insight Meditation Community of Washington[2]. You can also create a simple meditation practice using the

---

[2] Access free IMCW content at http://imcw.org/talks

techniques I teach in my meditation group by following the steps below.

Exercise: Simple Meditation

I recommend doing at least a ten minute meditation in the morning and again in the evening. It's my personal minimum requirement every day—you can certainly do more, but this is a good starting point if you don't already have a regular practice.

Find a comfortable upright seated position, either on the floor or in a chair. Allow your body to settle and to become still. Palms can be placed face up on the thighs for a more receptive posture, or the palms can be face down on the thighs if you would like a more grounded posture. Close your eyes and lift the crown of your head to the ceiling. Imagine that someone is pulling a string at the crown of your head, lifting your spine up nice and tall and bringing space in between each vertebra.

Bring your awareness to your breath. Each time we practice we arrive with a slightly different body than before—some days we are more tired, some days we are more energized. Just notice how it is for you *right now*. Notice how the breath is flowing in and out: Is it smooth and even? Is it short and shallow?

Now that you have observed its natural rhythm, go ahead and take a deep breath through your nostrils and all the way down into your belly. As you exhale, keep your lips lightly touching and exhale through your nostrils. Keep breathing smoothly and evenly, always coming to this practice with an attitude of curiosity and compassion. You may find that your thoughts are very active. When you notice a thought arise, instead of following the thought stream to see where it goes, or trying to "stop thinking" (which by the way is totally counterproductive), merely note the thought for what it is—thought—without focusing on its content. Simply note, "Oh, a thought," and bring your awareness back to rest right on the breath. This disarms the pull of the mind by disengaging from its energy.

Each breath presents a new invitation to re-arrive in the present moment. If you find that you have wandered off into a stream of thought (and sometimes it can be a while before we even realize we have left), don't beat yourself up about it and get mad. That's just more thinking. *It's totally natural for this to happen.* Have compassion for yourself and instead of getting upset, just laugh. How funny is it that as successful as we may be in our businesses, when we try to control our minds, we still fall for its tricks?

If you find that you are constantly coming back to the breath, great! That is what it is there for, to invite you to come back home to this present moment, the place where you are always welcome. Allow yourself to come home and rest in this present moment. If you find that your thoughts are so constant that it's not easy to cultivate any space or compassion for your effort, try to recite the following mantra, "I am here now in this." Sometimes setting our internal narrator to repeat a message keeps us from constantly leaving presence—mantra can be an excellent way to use the mind against itself.

As you breathe, bring awareness to your body. Sense all of the key areas of the body with curiosity. How does it feel in your heart, throat, head, and belly? If you feel any areas of tightness don't resist them. Just notice whatever sensations come to your awareness. If you encounter any areas that feel tight or uncomfortable, you can send your breath to the places that are calling for your attention. On the next exhale send your breath to any place that feels tight. Allow your body to show you where applying breath would be beneficial.

After ten minutes have passed, thank yourself for showing up and putting in the clock time to make this a priority. I trust that practicing twenty minutes a day for just one month will create results you never thought possible—meditation works in mysterious and amazing ways.

Let it Be

Meditation and mindfulness are best approached with an attitude of both curiosity and acceptance. This can be difficult for us Westerners—we generally respond to this kind of advice with "Yeah, yeah—that's all fine and good, but what are we going to DO about it?" In our culture, there is a heavy reliance on *doing* because we tend to believe that it's the only way to get things get accomplished. I invite you to consider a different approach, based on simply allowing whatever is present to be there. This approach involves functioning from a place where you know that consistently seeing something for what it truly is—clearly and without your own biases—will be far more beneficial for you than any "doing" will ever be, because the results last much longer.

The difference between *doing* and *allowing* is like the difference between someone who goes on crash diets to lose the weight quickly and someone who recognizes that cause of their obesity is the fast food they eat and drink for breakfast, lunch, and dinner. When the latter recognizes the truth and is ready to do something about it, the change in behavior will come from a place of love and compassion, and a perfect clarity that their habit is not in alignment with their goals. The crash dieter just wants the results at all costs—it may work quickly but it rarely lasts.

A great poem by the mystic poet Rumi, translated by Coleman Barks, says it best:

The Guest House

This being human is a guest house.
Every morning a new arrival.
A joy, a depression, a meanness,
some momentary awareness comes
as an unexpected visitor.
Welcome and entertain them all!
Even if they are a crowd of sorrows,
who violently sweep your house
empty of its furniture,
still, treat each guest honorably.
He may be clearing you out
for some new delight.
The dark thought, the shame, the malice.
meet them at the door laughing and invite them in.
Be grateful for whatever comes.
because each has been sent
as a guide from beyond.

Whatever tool works best for you to cultivate more presence in your life, I invite you to use it and use it liberally. There's a great saying that "ordinary things, done consistently, create extraordinary and consistent results." Building habits that remind you to return to the present moment will pay huge dividends for you as an entrepreneur. Even just sitting and breathing as you disengage from your thoughts, whether for a few minutes or an hour, can do much for your business.

Overall, any practice that brings more presence into your life—whether it's working with shenpa, taking sacred pauses, or meditating—will help you to more efficiently and effectively handle the challenges that come your way in all aspects of life. These practices assist you in cultivating certain traits of self-actualizers such as acceptance; a different perception of reality than others; fresh appreciation for life; prioritizing human kinship; seeking out peak experiences; humility and respect; and a good sense of humor.

Our desire to self-actualize and reach our highest potential requires that we be fully present for life's experiences. When we don't examine our triggers, we view the world through our own perceptual biases and therefore can't see things as clearly as we can when we are present. When we aren't seeing clearly, our blind spots cause us to make mistakes and create suffering, not just for ourselves but for others.

When we know how to deal with our triggers by acknowledging and working with them, we avoid wasting time repeating our unconscious patterns in our lives. People who are unable to be present typically have the same negative and frustrating experiences over and over again, just with a different cast of players. It's your friend who keeps dating liars, your coworker who seems to always have the worst assistant ever, your spouse who ends up betrayed by faithless allies. These people are stuck in patterns that keep repeating themselves until they are seen and healed.

Whatever truth will, cliché aside, actually set us free can only be uncovered when we are willing to get honest about what is happening inside ourselves. Even more importantly, when we are present and build the ability to hold this container of the now for ourselves, we can then begin to hold that same space for others and bring even greater value to our businesses and the world. Once we are present, we need to act—but how do we choose which course of action to take? How do we discern the difference between our unconscious patterns and the truth? By finding, calibrating, and learning to use our own inner compass.

CHAPTER 3

Inner Compass

O ne of the most important benefits of shifting into the perspective of oneness and learning to stay present is that these mindsets help us recognize and clear away destructive mental and emotional patterns. These patterns inevitably find their way into whatever we create, and can thwart even our best efforts as entrepreneurs. Integrating this new worldview also means we need to find a more reliable way of making choices—after all, a large part of realizing that we are running these unconscious patterns is accepting that we can't always trust our thoughts or perceptions. We must instead learn to find, calibrate, and use our own inner compass in order to make decisions that are free—to the fullest extent possible—of the influence of negative conditioning.

We often hear about people having feelings of imminent danger or warning that something is wrong, that ultimately prove to be true. Perhaps you've had this experience yourself—a "gut instinct" that ended up being more reliable than whatever thought process you used to make a decision. The more you practice being present in your life, the more these experiences will occur. Each of us has a built-in tool for navigating through life. Call it a sixth-sense, inner knowing, internal guide, the voice of the heart, gut feelings—it is a *felt* experience rather than a mental one. So what leads you to be able to not only sense the guidance you receive from your inner compass—what I consider to be your heart—but to trust it enough to follow it?

Even if you don't feel like you are currently following the directions it gives you, at some time in your life I am sure you can point to being aware of your inner compass.

Think back to a time in your life when you let your feelings direct your course. You may also recall—perhaps with much greater frequency—times in your life when you ignored or resisted that strong feeling because a voice in your head told you it was a bad idea. Maybe you simply talked yourself out of it using what seemed like perfectly logical arguments. Sound familiar?

For example, in the process of writing this book I experienced plenty of moments when my thoughts told me, "You can't write a book—you don't know how to write or what to write and no one would read it even if you did." Obviously I did not listen to that voice, because you're holding this book in your hands right now.

As an entrepreneur you have to know who you are taking your cues from—are you listening to your head, or your heart? When you're listening to that voice inside your head you have to consider, who is it that's really talking, and what do they really want? In this chapter we will explore some ways to interact with our thoughts and our instincts, and learn to discern the difference between the two.

Finding Your Inner Compass

Much has been written about "following your gut," and many successful business people credit their success to listening to their instincts, even in the face of conflicting information. So why is it that we have such a hard time listening to our own inner wisdom? I'm not going to go as far as to say that there's a conspiracy afoot to convince you to look everywhere but inside for answers, but it's not completely inaccurate either. To a large extent, Western culture does not place much value on following one's instincts, or really anything that involves feelings more generally. There is a strong societal pull in the Western world to look outside oneself to some external source of authority, whether that be God, the government, the media, or even our friends. One of the great unspoken assumptions of our culture is that someone else knows better than we do, and we should seek guidance from them. In business, we often find that we spend much of our time focused on our competitors, looking to see what others in our industry are doing so we can keep up—or even get one step ahead. While it's natural to seek validation and support from outside sources, and smart to obtain information from experts, most of us develop an unconscious habit of relying almost exclusively on external sources to make our decisions.

As the CEO of your business, this is especially problematic. When it comes down to it, *you* are the one responsible for making all of the decisions and setting the course your business will take. While you may be able to look to your board of directors, stakeholders, clients, and employees for input, ultimately the responsibility is on you. Ask yourself—from where am I getting my guidance?

For many of us, the answer is, "from my mind," or in other words, from logic and deductive reasoning. This is one of the curses of our culture. We are conditioned to listen to our thoughts, but relying solely on thought leaves us blind to the whole picture. If we allow only our mental understanding of things to guide us, we will inevitably have blind spots in our awareness, because our thoughts can be influenced by our unconscious patterns.

For example, remember the business I mentioned in Chapter 1 that looked great on the outside but was a mess on the inside? If you were looking to model your business after that company and you logically considered all the business they were doing, their reputation in the marketplace, and their labor costs, you would think following in their footsteps would be a wise idea—and you would be very wrong. But what if you considered the way that modeling your business after that company made you *feel*, perhaps you would get a much different message. Maybe you would feel uneasy, sick to your stomach, frozen in shock...that is exactly how my body reacted when I first met with the owner of that business. To make the best possible decisions for your business, it's always best to have as full a picture as possible. If you are using just your mind to make choices, you will be missing a great deal of valuable information—so much, in fact, that it can mean the difference between success and failure.

Please understand that I am not suggesting we completely dismiss logic: quite the contrary. The mind is a wonderful instrument in our tool belt that should be used when appropriate, but our thoughts should not necessarily be our default operating system. I started writing this book not because I *thought* it was a good idea—in fact, my mind had a lot of things to say to the contrary: "You have a baby, you're running multiple businesses; you need a vacation, not another project." I didn't push these thoughts away, though. I let them be heard and acknowledged, and then I chose to move forward based on the guidance of my heart. Learning to use your inner compass means taking a holistic approach to your decision-making—it means using both the head *and* the heart to make choices.

Like most entrepreneurs, the times I have not listened to the wisdom of my heart have been the times I kicked myself later. Have you ever felt like you intuitively "knew" the course of action you were taking was wrong, but just didn't trust that feeling inside? Or, have you ever made a decision out of fear of how it would look to others in your life, and had it turn out poorly? It's funny how we always imagine the things we *can't* do because of what people will think. Learning to listen to your inner wisdom begins with being able to identify limiting beliefs that take the form of your "inner naysayer," a voice inside you that keeps you locked into a small worldview with limited options for success.

Exercise: Hearing the Naysayer

Just in case you aren't sure what voice I am talking about, go ahead and think about something that you have always dreamed of doing and write it here:

_____

Think about your dream and finish the following statements:

1. I would have already (insert big dream) by now if it wasn't for

_____

2. I never have enough _____
to make (big dream) happen.

3. If I just dropped everything tomorrow and (big dream) people would think I am _____

4. I can't do (big dream) because _____

This exercise is especially useful because it illustrates, in your own words, some of the limiting beliefs you are carrying around with you all the time. To be clear, these limiting beliefs are patterns of *thought*—we are not working with feelings in this exercise. These beliefs may have emotional content attached to them, but at their most basic level they are simply conditioned patterns of thought that you hold about your life. They are precisely what your inner compass is *not*—in fact, these types of unconscious thought patterns are what obstruct your ability to make clear choices that are free of the influence of your patterns.

Most people never find out whether their limiting beliefs are even true, because most people don't have the courage to challenge their own limits and push their boundaries. As an entrepreneur, you already have that kind of courage within you—otherwise you would have never taken the leap into entrepreneurship in the first place. Now, we're going to use that courage to challenge some of your basic assumptions about the mind and belief systems in order to identify the voice of your inner compass.

You Are Not Your Thoughts

The more you begin experimenting with the exercises in this book, the more space you will start bringing to your inner world. Space is important in this type of inner work, because it's what allows us to step back and get a larger picture of what is actually happening inside us. Meditate for even a few minutes, and you will immediately find that there is a voice in your head; it is so loud, and so pervasive that you have likely mistaken it for who you are. In reality, it is simply your inner narrator, the ever-present mechanism of the mind that gives "voice" to your thoughts. The voice you hear in your head—the one that has a knack for zeroing in on your worst fears every time you're about to push a boundary or try something new—is not you. Take a few minutes and really listen to your narrator—it won't be difficult. It's always there, blathering on about whatever thoughts may arise, and has something to say about everything.

It's easy to assume that this narrator is you because it never shuts up, but in fact it is nothing more than a function of the mind. If you take the time to really listen to what it is saying, you'll realize that most of the time it's just spouting nonsense—it is talking just to talk. It expresses preferences and opinions that may or may not be yours, identifies and categorizes your sensory input, and dwells on the past or speculates about the future. The exercise from Chapter 1 about noticing your preferences also helps to illustrate this mechanism.

Recognizing that the voice in your head is not you is extremely liberating, and opens up the channels of communication between you and your inner compass. Because the narrator is only capable of expressing thought, it's not a trustworthy source of information and should typically be ignored as much as possible. In a business sense, it is extremely valuable to realize this about your inner narrator because that voice tends to talk you out of "gut" decisions that support growth and expansion—something all entrepreneurs want. The narrator believes it is protecting you by maintaining the status quo; it is trying to keep you safe. Knowing this allows you to disarm it a bit, because it's common to feel angry when we first realize we have been listening to a voice that has been blocking us from our highest destiny. You don't have to fight against this voice—that's impossible—just notice it, offer compassion to it, and do your best not to identify with it. This is something that is simple to understand, but it takes patience to cultivate the experience of recognizing yourself as something beyond your thoughts.

"I" am tired or "I" am hungry... who is the "I" really? Indian sage Ramana Maharshi became known around the world for his teaching on self-inquiry. These original teachings of self-inquiry were part of what is known as the "eight-limbed path of yoga" and they appear in the Yoga Sutras which were compiled around 400 CE. Maharshi suggested that seeing through this illusory sense of identification with the mind and awakening to our real nature of unbounded consciousness requires a regular practice of self-inquiry. Let's give one of his more basic but still profound methods a try.

Exercise: Practicing Self-Inquiry

Take a few moments to close your eyes and be still. Allow your awareness to rest upon your breath and follow the inhalations and the exhalations. Within moments you will likely notice a thought of some kind arise in your mind. Often the thoughts will feature "I" as the subject, as in "I think this self-inquiry exercise is stupid." As soon as you recognize this occurring, ask yourself, "Who am I? Who is the one asking this question? Who is it? What is it? When asking 'Who am I?', who is it that is asking and who is listening? Where does the 'I' come from?"

There are no right answers to these questions; you are not seeking information. Any answers you may find to these questions lie deep within, and even the most experienced practitioners of self-awareness and consciousness work can struggle with this. Our psychology is extremely complex and tricky, because you must use your mind to direct these questions of identity back at the mind itself. The purpose of this exercise isn't to come up with answers; the purpose is to short-circuit your identification with the mind. In fact, you'll likely find that your mind tries to answer with something like, "It's you silly." Respond with even more curiosity. Who is it that thinks this is silly? Who is it that is thinking this thought?

This exercise is designed to bring you into a wordless connection with your own consciousness. This is an experience beyond the concept or idea you have of who or what you are—this exercise puts you on the road to recognizing yourself beyond your thoughts. This alone can be one of the most profound shifts that consciousness can undergo.

While it's almost impossible to imagine a time when your mind is silent, it can—and does—happen. No matter how small these gaps may be between your thoughts, when noticed, they begin to reveal a secondary guidance system available to us. It is no less valuable than the mind, just slightly less vocal.

The Heart Speaks in Whispers

Connecting with your own intuition, this feeling-based guidance system, is not a process of the mind—it is a process of the heart. Logic and reason have no place in the heart. There is no making of lists, weighing pros and cons, or imagining potential scenarios based on a particular course of action. Tapping into your heart for additional information requires the ability to discern the difference between thoughts and feelings, and the results of doing so will sometimes surprise you. You'll have to be open and vulnerable with yourself, and willing to ask yourself tough, pointed questions and listen for the answer you receive—not just seek the answer you want to hear.

This still, small voice—this inner knowingness—has no need to bombard you with language the way the mind does. You won't find yourself kept up at night by the voice of your inner compass. Instead, the heart speaks in whispers—you'll have to be quiet and gentle in order to hear what it has to say. This type of work is often the hardest for entrepreneurs, because we all have a tendency to be oriented toward action rather than reflection and introspection. However, this can be some of the most valuable work you'll do as a business owner because it will help keep your business free from unconscious influences.

Think back to when you started your own business. Was your decision to become an entrepreneur totally logical, or was there something else driving you forward into the unknown? Starting your own business, while exciting, is really one of the most illogical actions someone can take. It involves a lot of risk, it typically requires far longer hours and more stress than working for someone else, and the results are far from guaranteed. Most entrepreneurs create a business because of a feeling, even in the face of the prospect of failure.

Another good example of this point is the process of falling in love. Assuming you've had the experience, how did you know you were in love? Did your thoughts tell you, or was it a feeling? When you fall in love with someone, you instantly find yourself with all of the information you need without having to think about it.

Your feeling is complete in itself and, while your mind may have plenty of thoughts about it, those thoughts arise after the information has already been received from the heart. This is how the heart speaks—from a place of *knowing* rather than *explaining*. Because the heart is constantly calibrating what is true for you in any given moment, it doesn't try to—or need to—convince you of anything.

The heart operates in a completely different way than the mind. Its wisdom is instantaneous, non-linear, illogical, and often paradoxical. While this may seem like a reason to ignore the heart, I encourage you to carefully consider the wisdom it has to offer whenever possible. As human beings, our motivation for any action we take, personally or professionally, is always based on a *feeling*. Any goal you have, any strategy you implement, any decision you make for your business or your life is not about what will happen when you get there—it is about the *feeling* you will have as a result. If you don't consider how it feels to make a decision, you may end up chasing your dreams down a road that leads somewhere quite different than you intended—whether you know it or not.

The Heart Speaks Through the Body

Read enough stories of highly successful entrepreneurs and you'll find one thing they all have in common is access to their own inner compass that helps them decide what is right for them in any given moment. Shifting to an approach in which you are following the guidance of your heart will allow you to see things you could not see strictly with the eyes of logic, which supports your ability to make better and more profitable decisions. So how exactly do you make this shift?

When coaching entrepreneurs, I often ask them how they feel about what is happening in their business. I typically find that they are far more aware of how they think than how they feel. Because of the bias against feeling in our culture, and the fact that entrepreneurs have a tendency to have very strong minds, most business owners struggle with getting in touch with the wisdom of the heart. One recent conversation with a client went like this:

"How do you feel about staying in this business and not retiring this year?"

"I don't have an exit plan, so it looks like I am doing this for another year."

"But how do you *feel* about that?"

"Like it's too late now to do anything this year. Maybe next year."

That's not a feeling, though—it's just another thought. There's a world of difference between thinking and feeling, and the mind has the capability to hijack your awareness by *thinking* about feelings instead of *feeling* them. This process is called bypassing, and the stronger your mind is the more vigilant you'll need to be to ensure that you are listening to your heart and not your mind.

It's easy to confuse thoughts and feelings if you aren't used to doing this type of work, and this confusion can keep you in your head without even realizing it.

Simply put, feelings are either emotions or physical sensations in the body—anything else is thought. For example, if I asked you how you felt and you said "I feel like a failure" or "I feel unappreciated," neither of those things are emotions or physical sensations, so they are thoughts. By contrast, feelings would be things like "I feel depressed" or "I feel full." The easiest way to tell the difference between the two is that feelings are uncontestable, while thoughts are. For instance, if someone says "I feel like a failure," you could say "You're not a failure, look at all the great things you've done." But, if someone says "I feel tightness in my chest," it's much harder to dispute—it simply *is*.

The heart is our inner compass, and the body is the access point for the information it has to offer. Remember when we talked about shenpa in the previous chapter? During "trigger" events, an effective way to deal with shenpa is to focus on the physical sensations in your body rather than the story playing out in your mind. Emotions all have physical sensations associated with them in one way or another—happiness and joy may bring a physical sensation of energy and excitement, while sadness or loneliness feels heavy or even cold. In order to connect with your inner compass, you must connect with your body. What are some of the ways that key emotions may show up in the body? Here's just a sampling based on the work I've done with my clients over the years:

Grief: Heaviness in the area of the heart

Shame: A sinking sensation of getting smaller, often with a sense of heat especially in the face

Anger: Pressure; heat; vibration; sense of propulsion

Fear: Tightness and clenching, often in the throat and chest cavity and heart center

Joy: Elevated; lifting upward; openness; warm as opposed to hot

Peace: Open and vast sensation, particularly in the throat and the heart area; cool sensation

Love: Uplifting; warm; open and loose; tingling in the belly sensation of butterflies; expansive

There are many more examples, but you can begin to get a sense of the difference between thoughts and emotions and their associated physical sensations. There is no way you can live your best fullest life or maximize your potential as an entrepreneur if you don't include the rich source of wisdom and information that is your body.

You might be surprised to learn that we repeat this pattern of confusion between thoughts and emotions in many ways, including our perceptions of our business. Often, the way we think about our business is not the way we *feel* about our business.

I had a conversation with a coaching client a few months ago who told me that she felt her business was really successful. When I asked her what, specifically, about her business led her to feel it was successful, she said, "The fact that I have been doing it for five years means it's been a success." When I asked her to tell me what she thought her business would be like in another five years she answered, "Well, I feel sick inside every month when all the bills come due. So I don't think I can actually keep it going for another five the way it is now."

This client "thought" her business was a success, and sure, keeping a business afloat for five years is by some measures a success. But her body was telling her that she felt sick about the state of her business and it reminded her of that monthly, if not daily. When I inquired about her physical sensation of nausea and tightness in her gut, she admitted that her business had lost money four of the last five years and she was really struggling with stress and anxiety. Together we worked on shifting her awareness to the whispers of her heart, particularly the way her body felt as she made business plans and decisions, and soon she began to see some improvement both in how she felt at bill time, and also how she felt about her business overall.

Again, it's not that thoughts don't have merit and value—logic has done many great things for us as a species and is great for solving many types of problems. However, your body is the final gate, so if you have a thought about your business and your body's reaction is negative, something is wrong. Your body is the ultimate litmus test for truth. This doesn't mean you will like the truth, just that your heart—through your body—will guide you toward it.

How then do we apply the wisdom of the body to our businesses? It requires stopping, connecting with the body, asking a question, and feeling for the answer. Let's try an exercise to test this out.

Exercise: Stuck or Free

Note: Read through the exercise first and then try it with your eyes closed with your awareness focused on the body.

First, let's bring to mind the feeling of being stuck. Imagine a time in your life where you felt stuck, like you didn't have the answer, like you were powerless and nothing you could do would free you from this stuck feeling. This could be a situation related to your business or your personal life, just try to remember every aspect of the experience you can—not just the story of what happened. After you have re-created this experience as if it was happening right now, and brought it into the present moment with you, inquire within. How does it feel in your body? How does it feel in key areas like your head, chest, heart, throat, and belly?

Got it? Now write down how it feels in those areas.

When I re-create the feeling of being stuck about the
_____ situation...

My head feels: _____

My throat feels: _____

My chest feels: _____

My heart feels: _____

My stomach feels: _____

Now, think back to a time in your life when you felt totally free. Maybe you were in love, maybe you were on a
beach sunbathing. Really bring that experience in to the
front of your awareness and then ask yourself how it felt
in your body.

When I re-create feeling of being free in the
_____ situation...

My head feels: _____

My throat feels: _____

My chest feels: _____

My heart feels: _____

My stomach feels: _____

Great! Now you should have a clear sense of what *stuck*
and *free* both feel like in your body—usually one feels
closed or constricting, like pressure, while the other
feels open and expansive. We've now calibrated your
inner compass and will be able to use "stuck" and "free"
to make decisions. Ideally, you want to choose the path
that aligns with the feeling of openness and freedom

whenever possible. When we are experiencing "stuck-ness" we are not moving forward—obstructions block our path, and difficulty lies ahead. If we set our compass towards growth and self-actualization, we want to use the feeling of freedom to point us in the right direction.

Now I want you to apply this tool to some of your current business decisions. Think of three things that you need to make decisions about, and write down a few words that will remind you of your choices (i.e. should I expand my company with outside investments; should I start this new venture; should I hire a virtual assistant?)

1. _____

2. _____

3. _____

One at a time, hold each question in your mind and then feel into the body. Avoid the tendency to try to analyze, label, or categorize; the mind is a wonderful tool, but we aren't using it here. Instead, feel into each question and ask yourself if it feels closer to the way that your body felt freedom, or to the way your body felt stuck.

Now, it's time to put this information into action. Show yourself you are willing to listen to your inner compass by actually following the guidance it gave you and then honestly reporting the results to yourself. When you decided to do (or not do) something because that felt more freeing in the exercise, did that decision move you closer to a feeling of freedom when it all shook out?

Learning to trust your inner compass and follow the wisdom of the heart is a process; it's a skill that is honed through the experience of using it in your life.

What Living in the Heart Looks Like

I can't think of a better example of someone who uses all of these principles in making her own business decisions than Oprah Winfrey. In the August 2011 issue of *O magazine*, Oprah talks about using her intuition. She says: "For all the major moves in my life—to Baltimore, to Chicago, to own my show, and to end it—I've trusted my instincts. I take in all the information I can gather. I listen to proposals, ideas, and advice. Then I go with my gut, what my heart feels most strongly. And I often tell friends: When you don't know what to do, do nothing. Get quiet so you can hear the still, small voice—your inner GPS guiding you to true North."

That's about as strong an endorsement as I've seen for listening to the wisdom of the heart, and is especially powerful coming from a billionaire media mogul and one of the greatest entrepreneurs of our time.

Living in the heart requires that we trust the heart's wisdom and accept the truth in every moment of our experience—no matter what—an opportunity for growth. Even with a strong connection to your inner compass, success is never guaranteed. In fact, the further you travel down the road that leads to your wildest dreams, the more likely you are to encounter uncertainty, disappointment, and suffering. Learning to deal with these feelings is critical on the path of self-actualization, because the truth is that we can make all the plans we want, but life often has other plans for us.

Life is uncertain. Nothing lasts forever. As hard as you try to reach your goals, you may still fail. And, as strange as it sounds, failure may be the best thing that ever happened to you. When growth is your top priority, one of the most powerful teachings that life can offer you on the path to self-actualization is impermanence.

CHAPTER 4

Impermanence

It's human nature to want to feel safe and stable. On Maslow's hierarchy of needs, the need for safety and security comes immediately after physiological needs like air, food, and water. These needs are absolutely critical to our well-being and when they are not met, we are not capable of progressing toward self-actualization.

The problem is, the fundamental nature of reality is dynamic, not static—change is, indeed, the only constant. Seeds become trees, and trees die and become fodder for the forest. Children become adults, and winter gives way to spring. Nothing in the world of form is totally stable, even down to the very atoms that comprise the physical universe. In other words, we live in a world that is inherently unstable, and therefore potentially unsafe and insecure. This understanding is one of life's greatest lessons—it is timeless wisdom hidden in plain sight. If change is the one thing we know to be true from our experience, then why do most of us resist it?

Instead of embracing impermanence and learning to feel safe and stable when things are in flux—which is the natural state of the world—we instead spend our energy seeking certainty and permanence, which simply does not exist. This is one of the most fundamental misunderstandings we have as human beings—our fear of change causes us to try to change the outside world to address our internal discomfort with the fact that nothing lasts. Resistance to change causes suffering, and the more we resist the more we suffer—we have an idea in our minds of how things "should" be, but life often has other plans. When we are attached to an expectation of how our lives will unfold, personally or professionally, we set the stage for disappointment and disillusion.

Our obsession with planning is a great example of how we try to mold the fundamentally uncertain nature of the universe. You think, "If I make a plan, then I know what will happen," but you really have no idea at all what will happen no matter how much planning you do. Deep down, some part of you knows this, so anxiety bubbles below the surface of our awareness all the time. Our response is a preoccupation with everything but what's currently in front of us—it's really nothing more than a way to distract ourselves from that anxiety. This future-oriented anxiety takes us out of the present in a vain effort to find certainty where there is none to be found. Yes, planning and strategy have their place in helping us orient ourselves toward our goals, but becoming overly attached to our plans—or the goals we ultimately seek—creates the potential for emotional pain.

Even though we may know conceptually that impermanence is the truth of our reality, we have a competing
instinctual need to see things as permanent because it
makes us feel safe. Constantly trying to box things up
into predictable and neat containers in our minds is a
coping mechanism for the unpredictable, chaotic truth of
impermanence. People shouldn't die. Businesses
shouldn't fail. Economies shouldn't collapse. We want to
maintain the status quo at all times because we believe it
will keep us safe, but how helpful is that belief to our
ability to make peace with our actual *experience* of life?

As self-actualizers already know, it's not very helpful
at all. Our unwillingness to face the truth of impermanence causes us to live in a constant state of denial, and
this leads to poor decision making. We neglect areas in
our life that need attention because they are changing, or
have already changed, and we simply don't want to face
it. As we discussed in Chapter 2, our obsessive avoidance
of the present moment is driven by the anxiety we allow
to fester inside ourselves, and this anxiety is further
fueled by our inability to accept impermanence. We can
usually skate by this way for some period of time, but
denial can only last so long—eventually, the proverbial
chickens come home to roost.

However, when we find a way to accept and embrace
the reality of change, we can turn it into a source of
power instead. We begin to find flexibility, moving *with*
the current of life instead of swimming against it. Our
planning for the future becomes less of an exercise in
avoiding our anxiety in a vain attempt to control the un-

controllable, and becomes an opportunity for real contingency planning. It all begins with coming to some basic sense of comfort with the reality of uncertainty. This chapter will show you how to get comfortable with impermanence and start building upon that comfort, allowing you and your business to thrive in a constantly changing world.

Accepting Impermanence

In business, as well as in life more generally, we typically resist circumstances we perceive as negative—a market that disappears overnight, a service that becomes obsolete, the loss of our biggest contract, the death of our co-owner, a health crisis, divorce, and so on. These unforeseen events are so uncomfortable and disappointing we just want to bury our heads in the sand or run for the hills. If only that worked! The problem is that resistance and avoidance just makes things worse. When you are in a state of resistance, of not wanting to face the reality of what *is*, you are not present enough to affect any meaningful change—in the situation or yourself. This is a poor recipe for self-actualization, and bad news for your life and your business. Whatever has happened requires you to be present to address it, to adapt to it, and to transform yourself or your business to flow with these new circumstances. Change is a powerful catalyst for growth, and the extent to which you are able to embrace change will determine the amount you can grow from any experience.

The antidote for the poison of resistance is the self-actualizers' trait of *acceptance*. You must learn to be present and accept whatever happens, whatever form the "now" is currently taking. Admittedly, this is difficult at first, but with practice we can learn to fully embrace this attitude in all areas of life. It's important to know that this is not about accepting anything that might happen in the future—this attitude is only about accepting what is happening *now*. It's also not about waving a white flag, or failing to take action. Accepting things as they are, in every moment, enables you to access your full power and aligns you with the flow of life; the opportunities are limitless when you create change from that empowered place.

When change and uncertainty have unforeseen or negative impacts on your business, your first priority must be to accept what has happened with as little resistance as possible, including whatever feelings and reactions it has caused in you. My best prescription for how to do this is a simple four word mantra that has gotten me and many of my clients through a difficult time: "This too shall pass." Repeating this powerful phrase has a way of anchoring in the core lesson that impermanence offers. The force of impermanence that has brought this change into your life will inevitably sweep it away by bringing more changes. Remember, the universe is dynamic and in a constant state of flux, so things that change for the worse will inevitably change again for the better—often in mysterious or unpredictable ways. The key to harnessing the power of impermanence is to remain *open*—open to change, open to new possibilities, open to the utter destruction of your dreams and the rebirth that will inevitably follow.

Embracing Impermanence

No matter how well we prepare, and no matter how much we follow wise principles for success, failure is always a possibility. It can be incredibly difficult to apply conscious principles when faced with failure because so much of our ego—our sense of self—is wrapped up in our drive for success. Being an entrepreneur demands that we take risks; it's one of the reasons success is so rewarding on a personal and financial level for an entrepreneur. Here, too, the wisdom of impermanence can save you.

Failure—and all of the difficult emotions that come with it—will pass, and can teach us powerful lessons about ourselves and our lives. The seeds of success are within every failure, if we only take the time and effort to salvage them and water them. By accepting the truth of what is, and by dropping unnecessary and unhelpful resistance, we free up our energy to learn the lessons available from difficult experiences. We can then choose to *do* something about whatever has happened, from a space of clarity and non-attachment.

It's easy to become completely neurotic about needing to find solid ground amid the daily chaos of our lives and businesses. Think about a situation you've encountered as an entrepreneur where something really important about your business is unresolved, like waiting to find out if you landed a really big client, or a book deal, or a new opportunity. What was your internal reaction to a situation that was "unresolved" for a period of time? Chances are there is something right now in your life that is unresolved. If so, ask yourself, how do I feel about it?

This is one of the places I struggle most. I can tell you that from my own experience that, when faced with unresolved uncertainty, there is a deep need for the mind "to know." In situations where something big is unresolved in my life, my mind starts to get all wound up, thinking about ways in which the situation might get resolved. Instantly, I am coming out of the now and thinking about the future. Or I might also find myself thinking about what got me into this situation, and start replaying conversations and emails in my head. Now I've dragged the past into my awareness, too! My mind is willing to try just about anything to get rid of this icky feeling most of us can relate to, the feeling of things left *undone*. It's like we just want to find a way to nail it down, to lock it up, to label it, to finish it once and for all—anything so long as we don't have to feel this way anymore. This is resistance.

The only way to break this habit is to stop resisting the fundamental truth that things are dynamic; it is to accept that *it's okay to not know*. We are able to transform the way we deal with the unknown into something life-affirming by acknowledging these feelings and saying to ourselves, "Yes, this is how it is—unresolved."

Exercise: How's it Going to Be?

Think back to a time when things in your life were very uncertain. Maybe you were waiting to see if a large client would hire you, or if anyone actually bought the product that you spent your entire life savings creating—whatever it is, think back to the period of time before you knew how it was going to turn out and complete the following statements:

The time I remember feeling really uncertain was when:

_____

I recall worrying about the worst possible things that could happen. Those potential worst case scenarios were:

1. _____

2. _____

3. _____

4. _____

5. _____

The situation was resolved when (how the uncertain became certain):

_____

Did any of the worst case scenarios you listed in items 1-5 above *actually* happen? _____

I won't say that the worst we imagine *never* happens, because sometimes it does. But, I'm willing to bet that most of the worst scenarios you imagined never happened. Most of the time, our anxiety-driven future projections never actually come to pass, and our fear of the future is typically much more intense than reality itself. The problem is most of us don't learn to recognize this pattern, and so we keep experiencing anxiety anytime we are uncertain.

If you answered "yes," then you received an even more powerful lesson—all of the worrying you did beforehand still couldn't protect you and was ultimately a waste of your energy. Did you survive and did you learn something unexpected from the experience? Sometimes going through the worst experiences of our lives shows us just how strong we can be. Are you still breathing? Then good news: the uncertainty didn't kill you and has made you stronger as a result.

The Only Way Out is Through

Whatever we are facing, no matter what we have been through, the path of self-actualization requires us to stand up and forge ahead. Heed the advice of Winston Churchill who said, "If you're going through hell, keep going." There is deep and powerful wisdom to be found in adversity—as I like to tell my clients, *the only way out is through.*

The most challenging times in your life are when it is most important to remember that whatever is happening, it is ultimately happening for your growth and evolution. If we can apply these lessons to our most challenging experiences, we open the doors to profound transformation in our character and sense of identity. We find deep reservoirs of strength within us that get us in touch with who we really are, and can re-engage with our life and our business with this new energy and power.

Planning for Change

As stable as your business may appear to be, the reality is that it's always changing, as are the circumstances surrounding it. This is truer now than it ever was before. Technology, the internet, and a globalized economy have produced a hyper-dynamic environment that is creating massive opportunities, but also massive disruption. Look at Nokia, the largest and most powerful mobile phone brand not very long ago. In 2005, they celebrated selling their one-billionth phone and the company was a shining star in many investors' portfolios. Just two years later, the exploding popularity of smartphones, led mainly by Apple's iPhone, led to Nokia's demise. Just last year, Nokia's brand name was officially dropped by Microsoft, which bought Nokia during its downward spiral. While you may not be running a publicly traded technology company, you can still learn from Nokia's lesson in impermanence—you can take nothing for granted.

Business owners who unconsciously cling to their need for stability easily fall prey to the unflinching constancy of change and may not anticipate major challenges their companies will face. When business is good, profits are great, and things are working like a finely tuned machine, it's a wonderful place to be as an entrepreneur and you should enjoy it. However, it would be a mistake to fail to prepare for the inevitable change that will come along at some point. A new product or service could render yours obsolete, or consumers might start to demand a new way of interacting with your business. An unexpected change in the cost of the resources you need to provide your product or service may erode your profit margins, or a key employee on your team may relocate.

You cannot anticipate every change that will come, but you can do some contingency planning. By staying alert to the changes in your industry and the broader economy, you can sometimes see a wave coming that is likely to cause disruptions for your business. Entrepreneurs that are comfortable with uncertainty are comfortable inviting change into their businesses, and are more adaptable when circumstances change that affect their business. I want you to be the kind of business owner that creates change by choice, even in the face of unforeseen or undesirable circumstances. A willful change in direction, typically in response to shifts in the circumstances surrounding your business, is called a pivot—and as an entrepreneur it's your job to look for these types of opportunities.

The Pivot

Learning how to pivot is essential for any entrepreneur who wants to stay current and keep their business successful within the current of constant change. The key is to learn how to proactively respond to changing circumstances as early as you possibly can, preferably before you *need* to change. The more distance you can place between the time that you see an opportunity to pivot and when it needs to happen, the better.

An example from one of my own businesses occurred during the summer of 2014. DC Elopements, a subsidiary of my wedding officiant company, was doing phenomenal business with same-sex marriages, dominating the local market. We were helping dozens of couples get married every month, everyone was happy, and profits were soaring. At the time, Washington, DC was the southernmost jurisdiction that allowed same-sex marriage, and my company was thriving due to a huge influx of couples traveling from the South to get legally married. Things couldn't get any better for that company.

I kept a close watch on the changes in legislature around the country though, and it eventually became clear that soon there would be many more states legalizing same-sex marriage. On a personal level I was overjoyed, because it was a policy change I strongly supported, but as a business owner I knew it would mean a dramatic decline in the revenue that DC Elopements contributed to my overall wedding business. I did not know exactly when the change would come, but I started to prepare.

First, I shifted my use of resources. I had been spending a lot of time securing more and more relationships with venues where I could set up out-of-town couples to have a quick, intimate, and legal marriage in DC. Now, I decided since I already had several locations to choose from, that was no longer a good use of my time. I took that time and devoted it to growing the aspect of my business that would not be disrupted—full-scale weddings, through my other wedding company, Ceremony Officiants. While some of these couples would still be same-sex couples, they would not be flying in from around the country looking for quick elopements. I invested more advertising dollars towards attracting local couples for full-scale weddings and spent a lot of time developing relationships with wedding venues in my area that could send me more referrals.

The pivot paid off. On October 6, 2014, the Supreme Court denied review of several states' marriage bans, and same-sex marriage became legal in Virginia and four other states. The next day, the 9th Circuit Court of Appeals ruled in favor of legalization in five more states. Two days after that, it was North Carolina and West Virginia. Overnight, revenue from DC Elopements took a major dive—more than 45% in less than a month—and never recovered. I was elated that so many of the couples who relied on our service could now marry in their home states, and by the next June the Supreme Court made same-sex marriage legal across the nation. Because I was able to see this change coming and took action to pivot my business, just as DC Elopements was drying up, revenue from Ceremony Officiants increased 104% as a result of my shift in focus. My ability to see change on the horizon, not panic, and acknowledge the situation by making new choices prevented the overall revenue of the wedding business from suffering.

While trying to predict the future has value, it's not nearly as valuable as being aware of what is happening now because not all change comes with a warning signal. This is especially true in business. Think of the classic example of Kodak—a multi-billion-dollar success story that dominated the world of photography for over a century. Since 1888, for more than 100 years, when people thought of photos, they thought of Kodak. When the trend started to move from film photography to digital photography during the first decade of the millennium, Kodak relied on their past success in the marketplace to predict that they would be fine in the future. They were unable to recognize that technology was going to significantly change their business, and did not take action quickly enough to save their company. After the fifth consecutive quarter of losses, Kodak announced that digital sales made up 54% of total revenue in 2005, marking the first time in the company's history that digital revenue exceeded film. The news came on the same day that the company reported total projected losses for that year could top $1 billion, due mainly to the restructuring that the shift to digital required.

In January 2012, Kodak filed for Chapter 11 bankruptcy. They liquidated legacy debts and patents they owned in order to survive, and by the end of 2013 the company emerged out of Chapter 11. The company still exists, but they aren't the Kodak you used to know. They don't really serve direct to consumer anymore, and instead focus on the film industry.

Kodak serves as a valuable lesson for business owners everywhere—adapt or perish. It doesn't matter how large or successful your business is, or how long it's been in business, if you rest on your laurels you are practically asking for trouble. Change is inevitable, and cultivating the kind of flexibility it takes to pivot your business when needed may make the difference between survival and failure.

In order to adequately prepare for change as an entrepreneur, you need to accept—and have some level of comfort with—change and uncertainty, and you'll need to do some contingency planning based on the unique needs of your business and your industry. One of the most popular tools for contingency planning is a SWOT analysis where you determine the Strengths, Weaknesses, Opportunities, and Threats present in your business. I actually used a SWOT analysis to see for myself that the change in my business was on its way. It looked roughly like this:

Example: SWOT Analysis

Strengths: I knew my strength was the reputation of my company to perform reliable, respectful, and lovely services. I was also located in a prime market, because our laws allowing same-sex marriage were long-standing and thus seemed more stable to same-sex couples than places like California, where Prop 8 had been overturned in short order. Also, we were the southernmost region that had legal same-sex marriage, making Washington, DC a prime location for southern couples to elope.

Weaknesses: It was only a matter of time before other nearby states or the Supreme Court made same-sex marriage legal everywhere, rendering most of the elopements unnecessary.

Opportunities: I started the company shortly after a Supreme Court ruling on DOMA made same-sex marriages recognized on federal tax returns and eligible for benefits, because I knew there would be an influx of people wanting benefits for their partners.

Threats: At any time, federal or state legalization could happen or marriage license laws could change in a way that would render my company less relevant to out-of-state couples.

Performing a SWOT analysis on your business is a great way to identify the places that need your attention. Often, when businesses run into trouble as a result of changing conditions, it's because they weren't able to see the ways they might be vulnerable. Taking an honest assessment of these factors will help you perform your due diligence as a business owner. While you may not be able to predict every change that comes your way, or ultimately affect the outcome even if you can, you'll be able to ensure that you've done all you can to prepare for the inevitable changes that come your way.

Exercise: SWOT Analysis

The SWOT analysis has been used by crisis management teams, businesses, and individuals. It is a popular tool that helps to define Strengths, Weaknesses, Opportunities, and Threats to your business, and identify areas that need to be addressed. Take a snapshot of your business as a whole by answering the following questions for each area:

STRENGTHS:

1. What do you feel are your competitive advantages over your most direct competitor?

2. What do others in your niche and in your industry as a whole say you do well?

3. What do your customers say you do well?

4. What skills does your company have that make it more capable of success than any other company in your field?

WEAKNESSES:

1. Where do you often get stuck in your business?

2. Where do your skills, products, or services need to be improved?

3. Where are you lacking efficiency?

4. What are the things your customers complain the most about? How about your employees?

OPPORTUNITIES:

1. What opportunities are present right now that you could capitalize on?

2. Where is something missing in your niche of your industry?

3. What are the biggest areas of potential growth for your company?

4. What are ways you could earn more revenue from your existing customer base?

THREATS:

1. Is there anything that could happen that could cause your business to become obsolete?

2. What new trends may negatively impact your business, and how?

3. Have you put yourself at risk of litigation in any way?

4. Is your business dependent on key individuals? If so, do you have processes in place to keep the business running if they were not able to work?

The Silver Lining of Impermanence

Learning to accept and embrace impermanence and change helps us to deal with tough times, and to be ready to seize important opportunities when they present themselves. Learning to embrace, and even look forward to, change also has many positive aspects that make the journey of entrepreneurship, and life, more fun.

Have you ever watched a movie where it was 100% clear what was going to happen at the end, and there was no suspense whatsoever? How about a football game where the score is 47-10 at halftime? These are not our favorite films or games to watch, and they can be downright boring. Half the fun of a movie or sporting event is the suspense of *not knowing* exactly what is going to happen, or what the outcome will be.

The same is true about life, don't you think? While the prospect of unpleasant change can cause fear and anxiety, the prospect of pleasant and enjoyable change is inspiring and refreshing. The power of a positive surprise or the payoff for hard work and planning can be so exciting, and could always be just around the corner. This way of thinking about change is powerful and gets you into a motivated mindset that prepares you to take advantage of opportunities that present themselves.

This is especially important for entrepreneurs—we want to create, and we want to watch our ideas become a reality. We want excitement in our career and, ultimately, the price we must pay for that excitement is the uncertainty of impermanence. It is a small price to pay for the thrill of creating a successful business venture that was shaped and molded by your very hands.

With this in mind, how do we take action toward our goals without being blinded by our unconscious patterns, or suffering when things don't turn out the way we expected? The best advice I've found for handling impermanence comes from the Bhagavad Gita, an ancient Hindu scripture written more than two millennia ago.

This ancient text depicts a conversation between Prince Arjuna and God, who has taken the form of his charioteer Krishna. Arjuna expresses doubt over what course of action to take on the battlefield, fearing that no matter what path he chooses it will end in disaster for his family and his kingdom. Krishna advises Arjuna to take the approach of Karma yoga—*action without attachment to outcome.*

This approach is the very same approach I advise you to take in all of life's endeavors. Taking action without being attached to the results of your actions—the fruits of your labor—is the only way to move toward your goals without creating suffering. By doing this, you can maintain a sense of flexibility, equanimity, and perspective as you make plans and execute them. By all means work, and try as hard as you possibly can to succeed, but let go of any expectations you may have of how things will turn out—the results just might surprise you.

Gratitude is the Attitude

Besides taking action without being attached to the results, one of the very best ways to approach impermanence—as well as plant seeds of positivity in your life—is gratitude. Because it's impossible to know what the future may hold, approaching life with a sense of gratitude helps to keep your priorities in check. For instance, anyone who has been seriously ill, or been close with someone who has, knows the reason why people say "at least you have your health." You can never count your blessings too often, and establishing a regular gratitude practice will help to keep your awareness on the impermanence and the many lessons it holds.

When I was working a great nine-to-five job at the local community college and running my business on the side, I felt exhausted and I could have easily approached my life and business with a lack of gratitude. I could have told myself a story about how I worked all the time and it wasn't fair that my business wasn't making me the same money as my salaried job, or how I was having to work eighty hours a week just to follow my passion. What entrepreneur hasn't felt that way once in a while? But how often have you given into it, letting yourself become trapped by your own cycle of negativity?

Instead of focusing on how exhausted I was, or how stuck I felt not making enough money to leave the day job, I put my energy into creating a gratitude journal. Each night, I wrote down at least five things I was grateful for during the day relating to my job. I knew that, in the life that existed in my wildest dreams, I no longer had a boss and worked on my business full-time. Yet in writing in that gratitude journal, I didn't begrudge the fact that I had a boss. In fact there was probably at least one entry a day that said, "I am so grateful that Christy is my boss. I am so grateful that she is kind, compassionate, and smart, and I consider her a true friend."

Even though I wanted to manifest a life for myself where I was working for myself and thus Christy would no longer be my boss, I wanted to do it from a space of gratitude. I trusted that if I was deeply grateful for all of the good things I already had, that I would be blessed with many more of the same even as my circumstances changed. Not long after, I did leave the job and Christy was no longer my boss, but I still had a boss who was compassionate, kind, smart, and friendly—and that boss was me.

Our appreciation for life, and our business, is simply a habit, and it's a habit we have direct control over. We can choose to recognize the inherent impermanence of life and be grateful for our business, watching the beneficial effects of our gratitude blossom, or we can choose to be ungrateful and focus on what we lack, cultivating frustration, despair, self-loathing, and anger.

Cultivating more gratitude in your life requires making a daily commitment to count your blessings. I'm obviously a big proponent of the gratitude journal, because it's a very simple but powerful practice for recalibrating your outlook from negative to positive every day.

Exercise: Your Gratitude Journal Ritual

Select a journal. You could create one out of paper you staple together and bind; you could use a standard notebook, a diary, or a fancy and beautiful journal. Whatever you choose should be something that feels sacred to you—choose a journal that feels worthy of the abundant gratitude that you will shower onto its pages. You should also select a writing implement that brings you joy. I can't tell you how much simple pleasure I get from my favorite Uni-Ball Onyx pen as it smoothly glides across the paper. This is a pleasurable exercise, so do whatever you can to make it as enjoyable as possible.

It's important to make this not just a routine that you'll complete begrudgingly in order to check off your "gratitude complete" box—you want to treat this like an honored ritual. My journal and pen have their own special home on my meditation altar. After my nightly meditation I take an extra few moments and consider five to ten things that I feel grateful for experiencing that day. Since you are just as focused on bringing consciousness to your business as you are your personal life, I would suggest listing five things you are grateful for in your work and five things you are grateful for in your life.

Afterwards, spend another few minutes in silence to just sense how gratitude shifts your internal feeling state. Check in with your body: How does this practice feel? At the end of the week, go back and read the gratitude you expressed during the previous week for an extra positivity boost.

You can make serious strides on your path to self-actualization by embracing both the negative and positive aspects of impermanence. Be ready to deal with whatever negative experiences may arise in your life, but be equally excited about taking advantage of the many opportunities that impermanence may bring. Doing so without getting caught up in attachment to a specific outcome, and maintaining a sense of gratitude for whatever happens in your life, will help you move forward toward your goals and dreams without creating suffering for yourself and others. Take action, and do so confidently. You must be bold.

CHAPTER 5

Boldness

Take a moment to stop and consider the types of people that shape the course of human history, the historical figures we never forget: Abraham Lincoln and his firm stand to keep the country united and to end slavery, a position that was fiercely opposed; Albert Einstein and his incredible imagination that led to a radical change in our scientific understanding of the material universe; Walt Disney, who would always say that he was in the "happiness business" yet managed to grow a huge entertainment empire around that simple goal.

There are many character traits people like this may possess, but one that they all share is *boldness*. A bold person is not someone who has no fear or anxiety, but is rather someone who acts in spite of it. A bold person does not ignore risks but considers them, and plunges ahead despite the potential dangers involved. A bold person often puts forward an unpopular idea, or one that is very disruptive to the status quo, and is often willing to

136 • LAURA C. CANNON

subject themselves to social rejection and failure as the price of greatness. Bold people can often seem pushy or aggressive at times because of their level of commitment to their goals, but these are the people who change the world. They change society, they change the way we see the world, and that is why they are remembered and celebrated.

Be Your Own Hero

While you may not be looking to make the same level of impact on the world as Mother Teresa or Alexander the Great, you will need to take bold action toward a committed goal if you desire to fulfill your life's highest purpose and to succeed in your business. Without boldness, the greatest song we have inside of us remains unsung. Without boldness, the true potential of your business will go unrealized.

Life is a unified whole—that is an idea we have explored in this book, and it is a powerful one. A complimentary idea is that you, and your experience as an individual, are a unique expression of that wholeness. While we are each connected to the bigger picture, like waves are connected to the ocean, we are each still a unique wave. The journey to self-actualization is one that requires us to both discover—and create—who we are and what impact we have on the world.

The truth is that the only thing keeping anyone from realizing their full potential is the inability or unwillingness to take bold action. One of the great visionary entrepreneurs of our time, Steve Jobs, said, "Life can be much broader once you discover one simple fact: Everything around you that you call life was made up by people that were no smarter than you. And you can change it, you can influence it...Once you learn that, you'll never be the same again." Each of us must be willing to become our own hero in order to realize our dreams. Knowing this is the key to unlocking your full potential as an entrepreneur, and acting upon it is the only way to get there.

Roadblocks to Boldness

We are all wounded in some way—no matter how happy your childhood may have been, you have had experiences in your life that were hurtful and left you feeling unsafe and unloved. While the level of trauma each of us experiences varies wildly from person to person, I have found through my coaching work that all people have some level of wounding around being loved, acknowledged, and accepted, and therefore have a distorted sense of self-worth in some way. These wounds can create many personality traits or patterns that severely inhibit our ability to be bold. Let's explore a few of the most common roadblocks to boldness.

Unworthiness

Many people feel bad for pursuing what they want in life, especially if they suffer from low self-worth. They may feel it is wrong or inappropriate to ask for what they want, or they may feel they don't even deserve good things. Thoughts like, "Who am I to make six figures when my siblings/friends/neighbors/children in Africa are poor?" will often cloud their awareness and stifle their motivation. If any of their actions causes difficulty or upset for another person, they will often beat themselves up or sabotage their own chances for success and happiness, consciously or unconsciously.

People who suffer from feelings of unworthiness have often created an unrealistic mental image of perfection that they are constantly trying to live up to, and will never able to achieve. This is extremely common in the Western world, where constant striving is the norm and messages of "not enough" are deeply ingrained in our institutions, our religions, and the messages we are bombarded with by the media and sometimes even parents or friends. At the core of unworthiness lies self-judgment—the tendency within us to be self-critical and, whether we know it or not, tell ourselves that we don't deserve to achieve the things we dream of.

People-Pleasing

Being a people-pleaser is one of the most common roadblocks to success in general, and is also a function of a distorted sense of self-worth. People-pleasing is a misguided attempt to find love and acceptance by trying to earn it from others, often by being extra nice or doing things for them. Trying to be liked by everyone, or trying to present an image of the "good" person we are, can often cause us to lose touch with our authenticity. There is nothing wrong with wanting to get along with others, but when that desire outweighs our own drive to achieve our goals, it's impossible to move forward with bold action.

The critical mistake that people-pleasers make is that they are solving for the wrong variable—they are trying to get something from others that they can only get from themselves. The love, acknowledgement, and acceptance that people-pleasers seek is something that can only come from within. Seeking it from external sources means accepting a poor substitute for the real thing— trying to find an external solution to an internal problem will never work. Ultimately if we aren't making decisions that are aligned with what is right for us, regardless of how it makes others feel, we will suffer.

Playing it Safe

If our sense of self-worth is fragile, or if we are addicted to receiving positive external validation, it can be nearly impossible to take any kind of significant risk—the fear of failure is simply too much to bear. We feel safer sticking to the well-trodden path than risking the failure that may lie down the road less traveled. Beneath our fear of failure lurks another terror: the fear of judgment—from others, but mostly from ourselves—and the shame that comes as a result. An overriding desire to avoid feelings of shame and embarrassment will keep you on the bench and out of the game.

It's critical to understand that playing it safe will make it impossible for you to reach your full potential in life or in business. Some situations simply *require* bold action, like expanding your business into a new area or hiring additional employees. Boldness requires the ability to take action in the face of fear—of judgment, of shame, of failure, of the unknown.

Pulling Weeds and Planting Seeds

If you are busy trying to play it safe, make others happy, or don't feel like you deserve to be successful, you will never self-actualize or evolve and your business certainly won't grow. These can be difficult traits to change, and while it's certainly possible to heal these wounds through therapy or various self-help techniques (which I definitely endorse), that isn't the focus of this book. Our attention, instead, is going to be on replacing these limiting patterns by focusing on what you *do* want, rather than what you want to get rid of.

I like to tell my clients that personal transformation is all about "pulling weeds and planting seeds." When you bring awareness to rest upon what is not working, as we have done in the previous chapters, you are pulling the weeds of your consciousness—the patterns and conditioning that keep you stuck. What we must then do is couple that work with really focusing on your desired outcome, planting the seeds of what you truly desire where those weeds once stood. Your inspiration and desire to move towards the things you want will help to till the soil and naturally remove the things that no longer serve you. It's an organic process that starts with recognizing and celebrating the unique expression of life that you are.

It's Okay to Be Selfish

"It's okay to be selfish," I said to my client, Gina. Gina was torn between being a successful entrepreneur, philanthropist, and mother. She was great at giving to others, but absolutely terrible at giving to herself. She had arrived for this particular session in tears about the fact that she was sick and needed sleep, and was so busy she couldn't even stay for our whole hour together. She would have stayed home and slept, she said, but felt too guilty to cancel. She looked exhausted, and needed to take some time to recharge. "I would love to, but I just have *so much* to do," she said.

Gina is a perfect example of the conundrum at the center of so many people's lives—not just entrepreneurs. In our culture, we are often so busy taking care of everyone and everything else that we neglect ourselves in the process. This is why there's been such a focus recently on "work-life balance"—we are literally killing ourselves with productivity. I personally believe that work-life balance is a great concept, but is incredibly difficult to achieve, and next to impossible for entrepreneurs because of the demands of creating and running a business. Forget work-life balance, what we need is work-life *integration*—a way to achieve our goals while taking care of ourselves in the process.

At the heart of work-life integration is a paradox—you can't really take care of anyone else unless you take care of yourself *first*. Thankfully, our newfound understanding of oneness has helped us create a fresh appreciation for paradox. You can't possibly operate at peak performance, personally or professionally, unless you put yourself first. You *have* to be selfish in order to take care of others. This is why Gina was so burned out—she kept giving even after all her reserves were empty.

If you find yourself working until you have nothing left to give, try to transform your attitude toward self-care. Recognize that achieving your goals requires bold action, and bold action requires fuel for the journey. Only you can fill the tank!

What Makes Boldness Possible

Famed American entrepreneur and author Jim Rohn once said, "You can't hire someone else to do your push-ups for you." Well, no one else can be bold for you, either. In those moments where something stops you, where you come right up against the edge of your own personal roadblocks, it is entirely up to you to find the strength and courage within you to be bold. To cultivate that strength and courage, it helps to develop a sense of higher purpose as a touchstone that can reaffirm your resolve in times of need.

Having a sense of higher purpose for your work, both personally and professionally, gives you the "why" of what you're doing. It's what you can hold on to when your courage wavers, or when obstacles seem insurmountable. It is one of the core principles of the larger "Conscious Capitalism" movement, and can serve to energize you, your company, and your customers.

Finding Your Higher Purpose

I love performing wedding ceremonies. It's a wonderful job—I get to meet amazing people and share a front row seat for one of the happiest days of their lives. When I started performing same-sex unions in Maryland, they weren't yet legally recognized, so the ceremonies were more about the couples' commitment to one another. I made it clear on my website and other marketing materials that I supported same-sex couples and was happy to perform these ceremonies. More than once, other wedding professionals warned me that doing this would alienate my straight couples—especially the more conservative types—and would ruin my reputation and my business.

Given the fact that same-sex commitment ceremonies weren't even legally binding, there seemed to be more potential for harm than good by promoting this service. I carefully considered the risks involved in continuing to openly promote this service on my website and marketing materials, and ultimately decided to move forward despite the risks. For me it was a simple choice, because I created my business with a very clear higher purpose. When I first decided to begin performing wedding ceremonies for people, I decided that my purpose for the business would be the same as my purpose in life—to spread love and consciousness across the world in as many ways as I can.

Was it a risk to continue marketing my services as open to both same-sex couples and opposite-sex couples? Perhaps. Maybe I did lose some business from those who oppose same-sex marriage and didn't want to do business with someone who catered to that market. But overall, my business never suffered as far as I could tell. I was able to continue spreading love with each couple that I joined. And, when same-sex marriage *did* become legal several years later, my company already had an established history of working with the LGBT community that resulted in a huge explosion of business.

Boldness necessarily begins with a strong sense of purpose. What are you here to do? What lasting impact do you want to make? How do you want to uniquely express yourself? These questions all start us on our path to determining why we want do anything in life.

Maslow's traits of the self-actualized person include a "problem centered" focus on life, meaning that they have a "mission in life." Often, our mission isn't clear at first—do you think that Martin Luther King, Jr. had a mission to end segregation from the time he was five years old? Probably not. Instead, his mission—and the purpose he fulfilled—was born of a combination of his environment, the platform he created through his life experience, and his own bold choice to dedicate his life to the higher purpose of equality.

If you feel like you already know your mission in life, great! Find a way to tie that mission in with the mission of your business, so you are keeping your priorities aligned in the same direction, doubling your ability to act boldly. If you don't already have a higher purpose you can dedicate your work to, not to worry—for most of us our mission is something we discover along the journey of our lives. When we start using the space of silence we have cultivated, being present for our feelings and using our inner compass to guide us, we are never far from finding the path that will drive us into an expression of boldness like no other.

Exercise: A Little Help from My Friends

Even if we are in touch with our inner compass, we may not always be able to see our own gifts or understand how we're already working toward a purpose. Often, it is others who reflect back to us the unique qualities we possess—we're often unaware of the best parts of ourselves, because they are so integral to who we are that they don't even feel special.

For example, public speaking comes naturally to me. I never thought that it was anything significant; talking to people had been such a part of my everyday experience for so long that I never even considered that it could seriously benefit me. After asking my friends to complete the following exercise on my behalf, I realized that it was truly a gift and not something that most people enjoy or are even capable of doing. Now I am actively using that gift to fulfill my purpose, and the universe constantly brings me opportunities for me to practice being bold by speaking in front of larger and larger groups. You can use your friends as a mirror for your gifts and talents as well by following these steps:

1. Choose five friends that you consider your closest allies (these could also be family members, but not all of them should be). These are people that have your back no matter what and love you enough to be honest with you.

2. Choose three peers or colleagues who know you well in a professional setting, and that you are also friendly

with. These are the people you wouldn't hesitate to ask for a testimonial or reference if you needed it.

3. Let these people know that you are doing an assessment for a project and that honest answers to the following brief questions would be tremendously helpful:

a. What is it that you really value about our relationship?

b. What do you view as my natural talents or abilities?

c. Complete the following sentence: When I think of (your name) I know I can depend on her/him to:

_____

4. Compile your data and begin to look for themes. Is there something that multiple people mentioned? Do they all depend on you for the same thing? Take any themes and begin to use your ability to investigate options through your body (i.e. what feels constricting and what feels like freedom) to see what answers are leading you to a deeper understanding of what your purpose might involve.

5. Now examine your own feelings about your greatest desires, and incorporate the themes from above to answer the following:

a. If I could be known for anything in my life, what would that legacy be?

b. What are some of my abilities and talents?

c. What gets me fired up?

d. I would love being able to get paid to:

_____

6. Looking at the answers from your trusted allies and colleagues, and your answers to the questions above, fill in the blanks to create a draft of your personal mission statement:

"I want to be known for _____
while using my abilities of _____
to get paid to _____."

For example: *I want to be known for spreading love and uplifting consciousness while using my abilities of intuition and speaking to get paid to connect with others and help them transform their lives.*

Access the wisdom of your inner compass as we learned in Chapter 3 to see if this statement feels like freedom to you. If not, sometimes a little tweaking may be necessary. Work with the language and themes until it makes you think, "If this actually happened, that would be awesome!"

Now that you have your higher-purpose based mission statement, put it somewhere you can see it regularly, such as on a screensaver on your cell phone, a sticky note on your computer monitor or bathroom mirror, or even in your car. Remind yourself of the impact you want to have and how you want to show up in the world. Priming your subconscious mind with this constant reminder will set you on the path to reaching your greatest potential.

The Two Biggest Pitfalls

After I had become a successful independent wedding officiant, I wanted to grow. I had a vision that would come to me in inspired moments, where I saw myself with a team of wedding officiants all performing marriage ceremonies in the personalized, love-based style I had created. At the time it was a big vision, and I did not really know how to make it happen.

All that changed one night at my mastermind group. If you don't know what a mastermind group is, it's a group of people (usually businesspeople or entrepreneurs) that meet regularly to provide support and encouragement to each other in a slightly more formal way than just grabbing coffee together. Think of it sort of like a board of advisors who help one another create goals and hold one another accountable for achieving them. These groups are particularly valuable for entrepreneurs and if you don't have one, start one! Best-selling author Jack Canfield has a great online resource[3] for creating mastermind groups.

---

[3] https://jackcanfield.com/images/stories/TSP-Mastermind.pdf

In my mastermind group I had been sharing my vision for a team of wedding officiants when one of the other members of the group blurted out, "Why not just create the training manual?" In some ways it seemed ridiculous. I had not hired anybody, nor had I even begun the process of hiring people. My business was just getting to the point that I had enough leads to support an additional officiant, and I thought I should find the right people first before I wrote their manual. Yet, the idea of writing the manual first resonated with me strongly. I felt a surge of inspiration along with a big green light from my inner compass, so I decided to take immediate action and I committed to my mastermind group that I'd have a training manual written within sixty days.

I committed at the point of inspiration because I knew my desire to work on this project would plummet the next morning when faced with the reality of actually writing a manual for my then-nonexistent staff which, of course, it did. I couldn't believe I'd opened my big mouth and promised to have this manual done in just two months! However, having that commitment not only to myself, but to others who I knew would hold me accountable, proved extremely valuable. There were moments when I struggled to sit down and write out all of my processes, knowing it was taking time away in the short term from me actually *running* my existing business. During those moments I reminded myself that doing this now would save me time and earn me even more money later. I remembered the support of my fellow mastermind members. And, mercifully, my own desire to meet deadlines and honor commitments got me the rest of the way through.

My manual was done within forty-five days and I brought on my first officiant within three months. Soon after, I had a team of eight people working for me, then ten, then more than twenty. Not long after, my company was serving most of the east coast and, in 2015, my company was recognized as the most popular wedding officiant company in the United States. It was auspicious that I made the commitment to create the manual when I did, because I could have fallen prey to the two most common pitfalls any entrepreneur encounters when taking bold action toward a goal—waiting for inspiration, and trying to figure out the "big move."

Waiting for Inspiration

We all love it when our action flows from a powerful sense of inspiration, an upsurge of motivated energy from deep inside of us. Being "in the flow" is always a great ride. But that level of inspiration only lasts so long, even when fueled by a higher sense of purpose. Achieving your goals involves taking consistent action, day after day, and you cannot expect to feel inspired every day. Sometimes the flow of creativity is going to feel blocked, or just dry up temporarily. So what do you do then? The remedy for a lack of inspiration is commitment and fortitude—in other words, you must make commitments when you *do* feel inspired, and then *keep* them even when that inspired feeling passes. Inspiration is often short lived, so the best you can do is take as much action as possible when it's around, and then use the power of your commitment to remain disciplined when it's not around.

Waiting to feel inspired can often leave you waiting forever—especially the larger or more complicated the goal may be. People who wait for inspiration, or time, or resources to work on their goals often leave the half-finished carcasses of their dreams laying in their wake. Think of it like trying to start an old car—sometimes you get lucky and the car just starts, but sometimes it doesn't. You still need to get where you're going, so you may just need to push the car to get it rolling and then try to start it. Often, you'll find that you can kick-start your motivation by *doing*—keeping your commitments even in the face of a lack of inspiration is one of the key ways to maintain momentum toward your goals.

Figuring Out the "Big Move"

Even with all the inspiration in the world, a big vision can sometimes lead to "paralysis by analysis." Some people bide their time, waiting for a massive transformative idea or the one huge opportunity that will make all their dreams come true.

Success never happens this way. Comedian Eddie Cantor is quoted as saying, "It takes twenty years to make an overnight success." Instead of staying stuck waiting for the perfect solution that may likely never come, focus just on what your *next* move is going to be, no matter how small it seems. Whatever you are trying to accomplish, there is always some type of step you can take to move forward. Take one step at a time and your "big move" will happen almost without you knowing it!

Risky Business

Taking bold action toward your goals involves taking risks—if nothing is at stake, it's hardly a bold move, right? Taking calculated risks is an integral part of being an entrepreneur, and is an aspect that a lot of people struggle with. It helps to realize that everything in life entails some level of risk. There is always a chance you will miss out on something or lose something in any action you choose to take...or *not* take. Even taking no action—staying put where you are or taking the "safe" path in life—is a tremendous risk. You risk never seeing what you were capable of, or what is possible for you.

Living a fulfilled life and running a successful business requires us to choose our risks wisely, but also to be willing to take on risks that scare us. Recklessness is not what we are talking about—a reckless person does not consider the risks at all and simply acts without any thought of consequences. This is dangerous, and often wastes resources. What I want you to do is take the risks *worth taking*. These risks are the price of admission to enter the life you dream of. When you aren't sure how to evaluate a potential risk, it's time to check in with your purpose again.

Ask yourself if the risk is worth taking in light of your higher purpose, and if the risk of failure outweighs the potential gains in success. My own success in business was catapulted by my decision to take a big risk. I was in my mid-twenties and had a deep passion for the wedding ceremonies I had been performing for several years. It was a fulfilling way to earn money and I absolutely loved working with couples on their commitment to one another, but the income I earned was not nearly enough to support myself financially.

This was okay because I already had a full time job—a *great* full time job—at a community college where I had an excellent salary and amazing benefits. I lived five minutes from my job and my commute didn't even require getting on a highway. Many people often told me how lucky I was to have such an amazing career and my parents were so proud of me.

As great as my job was, I wasn't satisfied. I had been working on figuring out my "why" in life—my purpose—and it had nothing to do with safety and stability. After tasting entrepreneurial success in college through my event production company, I knew wanted the freedom of running my own business and making my own decisions, and I wanted to feel passionate about the impact I was making on the world. My purpose, as I understood it at the time, involved love, spirituality, and relationships, so my small wedding business seemed like the perfect opportunity for me to start fulfilling my purpose through my work.

I was excited for the opportunity that my small business offered, but I was also terrified, and all of the traits that inhibit boldness reared their ugly heads. I felt guilty for not being more grateful for the amazing job I had landed at such a young age, I did not want to disappoint my parents, and I was scared to take the financial risk. I had just bought a home based on my steady and secure salary in higher education—was this really the time to give up a known income stream for an uncertain future?

Making the decision to leave my safe, comfortable career for the uncertainty of entrepreneurship was a difficult one. I used my inner compass over the course of a week-long silent meditation retreat, and ultimately determined that the risks were worth it. I would lose the security of a stable income, but gain the chance to align myself more fully with serving my purpose in life. Despite the fear of failure, I felt in every ounce of my being that the possibility of living my dreams was worth taking a chance on my business.

I didn't leap immediately without a plan—instead I saved as much money as I possibly could over the course of eight months and slashed my personal expenses. I poured every ounce of effort I had into my business, and within eighteen months of leaving my day job I was making more money than I had left behind. I was living a life filled with meaning, and the challenges of entrepreneurship were bringing out the best in me. Within three years, I was making double my original salary and never looked back.

You will inevitably face moments when you will have to decide if a risk is worth taking—if you don't, you aren't pushing yourself hard enough as an entrepreneur. Just deciding to start a business is one of those moments, but many more present themselves in the course of running and growing your business, such as spending a lot of money that doesn't have a guaranteed return on investment, hiring your first employee, changing your business name or structure, and expanding into a new market or service. When your purpose is strong and clear you will find the courage you need to take on the risks that are right for you. When you take bold action in the face of risk, uncertainty, or fear, you overcome the limitations of your patterns and conditioning, and healing occurs.

Why is this important? Why not just play it safe? Using boldness to make different choices in spite of our patterns is an active approach to healing our wounds and to helping us mature into the self-realized beings we are capable of becoming. In fact, the only way to know whether you've healed a pattern is by your actions—you either make a different choice for your life or you don't. Action is the ultimate test when it comes to personal growth, because only action shapes the course of our lives. As you know by now, when we grow as individuals, we become more powerful as entrepreneurs as well.

Pushing Your Boundaries

Do not wait to start. Take the higher purpose you've identified in this chapter and start working on implementing it in your business and your life immediately. Set goals, and commit to seeing them through, no matter what.

To set appropriate goals, you want to create goals that feel like a stretch. We always want goals that make us feel like we have to work for them, goals that make us feel at least a little uncomfortable because of how ambitious they are. For example, if you are currently making $100,000 a year, trying to make $105,000 the following year is not that much of a stretch, but setting a goal to make $1,000,000 next year would likely stretch you beyond the limit of what is currently possible for you. Goal setting is going to be different for every person—the best way to determine what goal is right for you is one in which you feel a little doubtful that it can happen, but not like it is truly impossible. If you would describe your feeling as one in which you would feel pleasantly surprised if it came to fruition but not shocked, then you've found the sweet spot. Use your inner compass to find the right goal by stopping, getting quiet, going inside, and asking whether each possible goal is right for you.

Your goals should be S.M.A.R.T. - Specific, Measurable, Agreed-Upon, Realistic, and Time-Based. For example: I will meditate for ten minutes in the morning and in the evening and will record my sessions in a journal.

These goal parameters are absolutely critical to your success. Any goal you set needs to have all of these components. Having a specific goal with no deadline is a wish, not a goal. Having a deadline without any way to measure success is a recipe for mediocrity. Having a measurable goal that is totally unrealistic is a quick way to lose your motivation.

Now it's time to create a goal using the things we have discussed so far.

Exercise: Taking Bold Action

1. Go back to the purpose statement that you created in the last exercise and write down a goal that can be completed quickly (within the next month *at most*) that would support your purpose. For example: *I will create a manual for the administrative assistant I've been meaning to hire.*

2. Decide what success would look like for that goal; be specific. You need to clearly define success because this will be the yardstick against which you measure your results. For example: *The manual will include step-by-step instructions for all aspects of the job description, including screen shots of each task they need to complete.*

3. Decide how you will measure your results against your specific goal. You need to be able to tell how far away you are from completing the goal, and be able to tell when it has been achieved. The easiest way to do this is to break the goal into smaller chunks that can be

used as milestones. For example: *The manual will be complete when I have written a list of all tasks associated with the job description, outlined each step needed to perform every task, included screen shots from any software that needs to be used, printed the manual, and put it in a three-ring binder on my desk.*

4. Secure the commitment of each person involved in making this goal happen, so everyone knows what the goal is, what it entails, and when it is due. Everyone involved needs to commit to their piece of the goal—if the goal only involves you, then you must commit to seeing it through. For example: *I commit to finishing this manual within the next thirty days. I need Cindy's help to get the screen shots for the software, and she has agreed to do those for me by the end of next week.*

5. Check to ensure your goal is realistic. Consider the potential issues that may arise—scheduling conflicts, lack of resources, and any unfinished prerequisites for your goal's completion. For example, you wouldn't want to commit to implementing a new web-based management system for your business if you haven't spoken to any software companies yet and have no idea how long an implementation normally takes.

6. Once you've completed your reality test, commit to a hard deadline. It can also be helpful to create smaller deadlines for the intermediary steps in your goal, so you will know whether you are falling behind. For example: *I commit to finishing this manual in the next thirty days. I will have the list of tasks done by Day Seven, the steps out-*

lined and typed out by Day Fourteen, the document compiled and with the screen shots by Day Twenty-one, and the whole thing completed, printed, and on my desk by Day Twenty-nine.

Start Now

You may be familiar with the Zen saying, "Leap first and the net will appear." This often gets misunderstood to mean that you should simply have blind faith and trust that if you follow your purpose, even when it doesn't seem possible, things will all work out. In reality, once you are clear on your purpose, you can use that touchstone to make a bold plan that involves just the right mix of planning and jumping.

I suggest following the Arab proverb that says, "Trust in God, but tie your camel." Yes, there is an amount of faith that must be present when you are following your heart. However, as soon as you move into making decisions without logic involved at all, you can expect that you'll be faced with decisions that may align with your purpose but have no realistic chance of success. "Trust in God" asks you to surrender to the elements of your life that are beyond your control, like the outcome of your actions. After all, it's entirely possible that, despite your best efforts, you may fail or you may end up with a completely different outcome than you initially expected. The "tie your camel" part means that you still need to be responsible in the way you operate, taking calculated risks and measuring your results.

Boldness requires action. There is no way around this. We have so far learned several foundational tools and concepts that will propel you forward on your path to self-actualization and business success. Doing all that work, however, is like collecting the kindling and wood for a fire. It needs a spark before it can become a flame. Action is that spark—the match that you'll use to actually start the fire burning in your life.

Many people live unfulfilled lives because they never act on their urges and desires. They may know their purpose and be able to feel the pull of their inner compass, but instead of taking action they wait for the right time or the right conditions. Fortune favors the bold—align your purpose, your goals, and your unique gifts and take action, now.

It's up to you to create the conditions for your success using the tools in this book, and you must find a way to integrate your personal growth goals with your business goals in order to achieve both simultaneously. This multi-faceted approach to life and business becomes infinitely easier when everything is in *alignment* – when doing good for yourself is also good for your business, and good for the rest of the world as well. Creating these types of win-win scenarios puts you at the heart of a new movement in the business world, one in which the generation of wealth is only one of many purposes your business can serve. Building your life, and your business, around the concept of *service* will allow you to create from a space of alignment, and transform not only your life but others' lives as well.

CHAPTER 6

Service

While self-actualization—the realization of our highest potential—rests at the top level of Maslow's hierarchy of needs, Maslow later added yet another level that he labeled "*self-transcendence.*" In 1961, nearly twenty years after introducing the hierarchy of needs in his paper *A Theory of Human Motivation*, Maslow wrote, "...the greatest attainment of identity, autonomy, or selfhood is itself simultaneously a transcending of itself, a going above and beyond selfhood. The person can then become relatively egoless."

At the highest level of consciousness, we recognize that what we do unto others we also do unto ourselves—the illusion of separateness dissolves and oneness becomes our primary experience. Maslow ultimately came to the same conclusion as the sages, gurus, and mystics of the East—that once you've reached this level and you've achieved all you possibly can for yourself, the only way to serve our highest purpose is to place ourselves in service to others.

In this book, we've explored the underlying oneness and interconnectedness of the universe, found our way into the boundless capacity of the present moment, and embraced the inherent impermanence of this experience. We've learned to use the body as an instrument to inform our decision-making, to align ourselves and our businesses with a higher purpose for maximum efficiency, and to take bold action toward our goals. In this final chapter, we're going to chart a path to the future—for ourselves, our businesses, and our society—through service.

Broadening our Concept of Service

Imagine what it would be like if anytime someone had an interaction with your business it eased their suffering in some way. Imagine how many people would feel drawn to work with you if they knew that by doing so, they would come away having benefited in some tangible way from your encounter?

Traditional capitalism is motivated primarily by profit, and the beneficiaries of a company's efforts are its shareholders—everything else is secondary. This narrow-minded approach may be incredibly effective at delivering wealth to a business' investors, but we are now beginning to realize that it has some serious drawbacks as well. Environmental pollution, dangerous working conditions, resource-motivated wars, and the undue influence of large corporations on our democratic systems are all results of the profit-first model of traditional capitalism. If humanity is to have any chance at survival, we must find a new way forward.

If your business is successful in any way, it touches the lives of many people—whether they are customers, employees, vendors, suppliers, or investors—as well as affects the community and the environment. A more holistic approach to capitalism recognizes that everyone and everything that your business affects is, in essence, a stakeholder in your business. It's no longer enough to focus solely on profit without considering the relationship your business has with the people that interact with it, or the effect it has on the world. Orienting your business toward service means recognizing that your company is not an isolated entity—it exists in a broader ecosystem that involves all stakeholders, each with their own set of needs.

Reflecting on how your business actually helps satisfy these stakeholders' needs is just another way to fan the fire of motivation that you have to run your business successfully. But this extends to more than just your clients or customers. What about your employees or contractors? And how about the other professionals you interact with both in and outside of your particular niche? These people are also part of your industry's community, not to mention the greater community of entrepreneurs. Did you ever think about how your business can serve them too?

When I designed my first training manual I put a lot of thought into ensuring my officiants could show up at any venue and perform their job without creating any extra hassle or drama for the wedding planners and co-ordinators. Approaching the process of delivering our services by focusing on the needs of the people we work with helped me prepare my officiants for anything they might encounter. It also made it so the other professionals we worked with immediately recognized our officiants were different than the ones they had worked with in the past. We cultivated an attitude of "How can I help you?" which was much different than other officiants, who were asking, "Can you help me?" You can imagine how this positively impacted our referral rate, not to mention the halo effect influencing the overall experience of the couples who hired us.

As a conscious entrepreneur, these kinds of relationships must remain at the core of your decision-making. This means being aware of the consequences of any actions your business takes, and making choices that reflect the values and higher purpose of your company. In their bestselling book *Conscious Capitalism*, authors John Mackey and Raj Sisodia write, "You cannot have a conscious business without conscious leadership. Conscious leaders are motivated primarily by service to the firm's higher purpose and creating value for all stakeholders." This could not be truer. As you progress on your journey to becoming an ever-more conscious entrepreneur, you will find yourself rethinking what role service has in your business and your life.

Exercise: Service in Action

Earlier in this book, you made a purpose statement for yourself as an entrepreneur. This statement aligns your higher purpose as an individual with the work you do. Keeping this in mind, how could you refocus the purpose or mission statement of your business to be oriented toward service? While donating a portion of your profits to a worthy cause is wonderful, think about all of the lives your business touches and how they are affected by your company. How could your business be of service to those people? How could it make the world a better place in some way?

After some brainstorming, list three ways in which your company could be of more service to its various stakeholders:

1. _____

2. _____

3. _____

Choose one of these that you could take action on in the next six months, and commit to implementing it in your business. Remember—bold action toward a stated goal is the only thing that creates change in the world!

It Doesn't Take Much to Make a Difference

Sometimes people feel like they need to have a lot to give in order to give back, as if doing good in the world is something reserved only for those with the deepest pockets. Nothing could be further from the truth. In fact when I was twenty-five years old I started my own personal "Do What You Love" fund with my dearest friend, Tim. One night we were talking about how grateful we were to have both had support in our journey to doing what we love. In fact, the first business I ever started in college (the production company I mentioned in the introduction) was funded by a $3,500 loan from my father. I could not have set up my first event without that money and his belief that I could do it. So Tim and I decided that we would pool our resources in order to give someone else the same opportunities we'd had. We each saved a bit of money every month and deposited it into an account. Within a year we had saved $1,000 in the "Do What You Love" fund.

We continued to build the account, and five years later the first opportunity came for us to help someone do what they loved. A mutual friend who was an amazing musician had been struggling desperately. Every penny she had went to the most basic living needs. She knew that to be able to make a career out of being a musician she needed to release her first album, but with all her time going toward the flute lessons she taught and paying for her expenses she did not have the resources to make it happen. She was living out of her car and staying at friends' houses when we gifted her with the few thousand dollars we had in our fund—not a huge amount, but enough to allow her to get what she needed to make the album, and it was the seed of a crowdfunding campaign where other people contributed to supporting her big dream.

Three years later our dear friend Angela is now releasing her second album and she no longer gives flute lessons or struggles to make ends meet. Instead, she hosts music workshops and retreats at her new sanctuary in the mountains, with her new wife! Just knowing that we played some small part in that, and watching how that love has now spread is truly incredible and fulfilling. She's helping other aspiring musicians do what she did and working to pay it forward. It's also motivated me to continue to find new ways to do good in the world and to serve others through my business, both directly and indirectly.

A Movement for the Future

Times are changing quickly in the business world, and old paradigms are shifting toward a more holistic, conscious approach to capitalism. This movement reflects a broader shift in our society toward higher consciousness—younger generations are more tolerant and more socially responsible than any other in human history. It's easy to see these shifts reflected in changing societal norms, whether it's attitudes toward corporate social responsibility, racial justice, or gender and sexual identity.

According to recent reporting from the Pew Research Center, the Millennial generation has now surpassed the Baby Boomers as the largest generation by population, and has overtaken Gen Xers as the largest generation in the U.S. labor force. Millennials are generally optimistic and socially conscious, and expect their employers and the companies they do business with to act in socially conscious ways. Until recently, it was enough for corporations to engage in charitable giving as a way to demonstrate social responsibility, but now the expectations are even higher.

Young people recognize that there is a difference between *giving back* and *doing good* in the world, and their expectations now reach beyond the traditional PR-driven model of corporate social responsibility. Moving forward, the world's best companies will need to demonstrate that they are actually making the world a better place in order to stay on top. In their groundbreaking 2007 bestseller, *Firms of Endearment: How World-Class Companies Profit from Passion and Purpose*, authors Jagdish Sheth, David B. Wolfe, and Raj Sisodia outline a compelling case for the future of business—one in which companies make a difference in the world *and* make a fortune in the process. Some of the world's top companies, like Whole Foods, Southwest Airlines, Costco, The Container Store, and Google are leading the charge of this new and exciting movement dubbed "Conscious Capitalism."

If you haven't yet read the book *Conscious Capitalism* by John Mackey and Raj Sisodia, I highly recommend you do so. This book, *The Conscious Entrepreneur*, has focused primarily on *you* as the entrepreneurial driver and leader of your business, and on how your personal growth and business success are deeply intertwined. In *Conscious Capitalism*, Mackey and Sisodia take the next step, outlining a new approach to business practices based on four tenets—higher purpose, stakeholder integration, conscious leadership, and conscious culture and management. Implementing the approaches outlined in both books is a powerful one-two punch that will transform your business into a force for good in the world, one with a bright and sustainable future.

Leadership Begins with You

When you are called to start a business, whether you know it or not, you are responding to a deep, inner need to move toward self-actualization—to reach your highest potential. Not everyone hears the call to become an entrepreneur, and fewer still act upon it—just by doing so, you have self-selected into a unique group of people and you need to realize that you are uncommon. You're willing to take on a huge challenge that also provides you with incredible opportunity, and one of those opportunities is to help others and make a difference in the world. Embracing this opportunity will align your work as an entrepreneur with the path of self-actualization, and allow you to use your business as a vehicle for personal growth.

In this book we've discussed all the myriad ways your unconscious patterns and emotional wounding can affect your decision-making as the leader of your business, sometimes with disastrous results. Transformational leadership first requires personal transformation, and you must never forget that your business is merely a reflection of you.

Make a commitment right now to continuing on this path, to pushing your own edge and stepping out of your comfort zone, to doing the hard work required to heal your wounds and shift your perceptual biases. Use your work as an opportunity to learn and grow—this is the highest expression of work-life integration. As Eckhart Tolle said, "Life will give you whatever experience is most helpful for the evolution of your consciousness. How do you know this is the experience you need? Because this is the experience you are having at this moment."

True happiness doesn't come from whitewashing your experience with hollow positivity, but from accepting the paradox of existence. You must embrace all of life's various experiences as an opportunity for growth, knowing you can handle anything that comes.

Love is at the Core

As human beings, we may be motivated by many different things, but at the heart of our deepest desires lies the feeling we wish to experience—*love*. Love can take many forms and be expressed in many ways, but love is always at the core of whatever drives us. Even our motivation for self-actualization and self-transcendence is motivated by love for ourselves and love for others.

I learned this lesson very powerfully while volunteering with a hospice organization and offering support to people at the end of their lives. These people came from many different backgrounds in life—professionals such as doctors or lawyers, housewives, immigrants who had just come to America—but all of them shared something in common. Despite their varied life stories, the most important thing to them as death approached was the presence, or absence, of love in their lives. They would talk about the significant relationships they'd had, loved ones who had already passed or those they would be leaving behind. Or, they would talk about someone they loved with whom they'd had a falling out, or had an unresolved dispute. These relationships would be troubling to them, and at the end of their lives, many of them expressed great regret over not working harder to put differences aside with people they loved.

I once had the opportunity to sit with a dying executive who had created a company that you would likely recognize. Let's just say that he had plenty to be proud of and plenty he could have shared with me about what it was like to create such a successful business. Yet, I had no idea *who* he was until after he died and a nurse told me about his incredible success as an entrepreneur. Despite talking with him at length several times, I never once heard about his business—I heard about his love. I heard about it in the form of the peak experiences he had in his life, those moments when he felt closest to what he described as God. I heard about the love he felt in his deep interpersonal relationships. I heard about it in stories he told of his family, his wife, his children, his grandchildren. I experienced it by watching his fresh appreciation for the acts of love that he was still being greeted with, even as he lay dying.

I was already an entrepreneur by this time and running my own business, and I made my business success my top priority—as most entrepreneurs do. I took the love in and around me for granted because I was climbing the ladder of success. As far as I was concerned, love was for relationships and didn't have a place in the cutthroat world of business. Those years of volunteer work in hospice profoundly changed me. They allowed me to see with the clarity that only mortality can bring—that at the end of your life, it is only the love you've received and given, or failed to give and receive, that matters.

As an entrepreneur and the leader of a conscious business, you have the opportunity to spread love through your company and impact the lives of everyone that interacts with you and your business. The relationships that you have with your staff members, and the relationships that your business has with everyone it touches, hold the potential for love and transformation. When you commit to using your business as a vehicle for personal transformation, it has the magical effect of catalyzing opportunities for growth in others.

Act Now

Oprah Winfrey, in a 2014 interview at the Stanford Graduate School of Business, said, "It's so important that you have leaders who are self-actualized and understand what [their] contribution to change the world can be. You can only do that if you know yourself. You cannot do it unless you take the time to know who you are and why you are here...and you cannot fulfill it unless you have a level of self-awareness—to be connected to what is the inner voice or the instinct—that allows you to make the best decisions for yourself."

This book has given you an overview of the journey ahead and a few tools to get you started, but only you can walk the path of your own liberation. It is not enough to read about these principles and practices and merely comprehend them—they must be experienced in your everyday life in order to be understood. Every action you take toward your own healing and growth will pay dividends for your business, and have a positive effect on the lives of everyone you come into contact with. Mahatma

Gandhi was right; you must *be* the change you wish to see in the world.

Have the courage to dream wildly and take bold action toward creating something beautiful, for yourself and for your business. Entrepreneurs shape our society. We create our culture, and we influence the world by creating new products, services, and opportunities that change people's lives. Ultimately, conscious entrepreneurship is about finding creative, synergistic solutions for your business, where problems are solved on multiple levels simultaneously, and create win-win scenarios for everyone involved.

My deepest desire is that this book will serve as a tool to aid you on your journey to becoming the conscious entrepreneur you were always meant to be.

Additional Resources

This is a list of other resources that have helped me tremendously on my journey and that I find myself continuously recommending to clients. I also invite you to visit my website, http://lauraccannon.com, and to subscribe to my mailing list for additional resources and content to support you in your journey to becoming a Conscious Entrepreneur.

Books

Be As You Are: The Teachings of Sri Ramana Maharshi, by Sri Ramana Maharshi, edited by David Goodman (New York, NY: Penguin Books, 1989)

Conscious Capitalism: Liberating the Heroic Spirit of Business, by John Mackey & Rajendra Sisodia (Boston, MA: Harvard Business Review Press, 2014)

Delivering Happiness, by Tony Hseih (New York, NY: Grand Central Publishing, 2013)

Expectation Hangover: Overcoming Disappointment in Work, Love and Life, by Christine Hassler (Novato, CA: New World Library, 2014)

Power vs. Force, by David Hawkins (Carlsbad, CA: Hay House 2013)

Radical Acceptance, by Tara Brach (New York, NY: Bantam Books, 2004)

Reinventing You: Define Your Brand, Imaging Your Future, by Dorie Clark (Boston, MA: Harvard Business Review Press, 2013)

Stand Out; How to Find Your Breakthrough Idea and Build a Following Around It, by Dorie Clark (New York, NY: Penguin Publishing, 2015)

Steering by Starlight: Find Your Right Life, No Matter What, by Martha Beck (New York, NY: Rodale, 2009)

The Bhagavad Gita: A Classic of Indian Spirituality, translated by Ecknath Easwaran (Tomales, CA: Nilgiri Press, 2009)

The E-Myth Revisited: Why Most Small Businesses Don't Work and What to Do About It, by Michael E. Gerber (New York, NY: HarperCollins Publishing, 2001)

The Power of Now, by Eckhart Tolle (Novato, CA: New World Library, 2010)

The Presence Process, by Michael Brown (Vancouver, Canada: Namaste Publishing, 2010)

The Success Principles, by Jack Canfield (New York, NY: Harper Collins, 2005)

The Tibetan Book of Living and Dying, by Sogyal Rinpoche (New York, NY: Harper Collins, 2009)

The Untethered Soul, by Michael Singer (Oakland, CA: New Harbinger Publications, 2007)

The War of Art, by Steven Pressfield (New York, NY: Black Irish Entertainment, 2011)

Audiobooks

Do You Do It, or Does It Do You? How to Let the Universe Meditate You, by Alan Watts (Louisville, CO: Sounds True Publishing, 2005)

Don't Bite The Hook: Finding Freedom from Anger, Resentment and Other Destructive Emotions, by Pema Chödrön (Boston, MA: Shambhala Audio, 2007)

Websites

Audio and Video Meditation Talks from Tara Brach and the Insight Meditation Community of Washington: http://www.imcw.org/Talks

High vibrational music and mantras: http://www.sacredvalleytribe.com/medicine-songs/

About the Author

The past fifteen years of Laura's life have been a period of deep self-exploration, teaching, healing, and love that has involved apprenticing and studying with spiritual teachers, ministers, healers and shamans from across the globe. At the same time, she has been balancing her spiritual practice with a busy and successful professional life including entrepreneurship, leadership training, and professional public speaking. Laura currently owns several businesses, including Ceremony Officiants™, one of the largest and most successful wedding officiant companies in the United States. She is also the founding president of the International Association of Professional Wedding Officiants.

Ordained as a nondenominational minister in 2003, Laura has been ministering and coaching individuals and couples for over a decade. She holds a B.S. from Towson University and an M.A. in Human Sciences from Hood College with a specialization in Thanatology and Grief Counseling. A lover of all things that blend the practical and the spiritual, Laura is also a 200hr RYT yoga instructor and meditation teacher.

Learn more at http://lauraccannon.com

Made in the USA
Middletown, DE
22 May 2016